THE
PORTS H
E

WN

Down Memory Lane

Down Memory Lane I linger long,
Till evening shadows fall,
To dream of golden days bygone,
And radiant hours recall.

MILESTONE PUBLICATIONS ®

Phototypesetting by Inforum Ltd, Portsmouth
Printed in Great Britain by
Conifer Press, Fareham, Hampshire.

Published by
Milestone Publications
62 Murray Road
Horndean
Hants PO8 9JL

First impression 1984
Reprinted 1985

British Library Cataloguing in Publication Data

Brown, Ron, *1932–*
Portsmouth Emporium.——(Down memory lane; 12)
1. Stores, Retail——England——Portsmouth
(Hampshire)——History
I. Title II. Series
381′.1′09422792 HF5429.6.G7

ISBN 0–903852–43–8

With the number of leisure hours now available to most people these days and perhaps with the prospect of even more in the future, I think it would be reasonable to assume that the home entertainment industry is riding on the crest of a wave in the 1980s. The wonder of television has been married to the marvel of video, not only providing the advantage of being able to view movies and programmes of our own choice, but also a vast selection of games in the futuristic mould that may be played from the comfort of our armchairs. And yet, if one thinks about it, most folk possess the finest built-in entertainment machine that they are likely to encounter, and all for free! I refer, of course to the human memory that is planted in our craniums.

Our memories are indeed wonderful instruments, if you concentrate enough it is quite likely that you will recall names and places from the past that you thought you had long since forgotten. For the ultimate in nostalgic pleasure, I suggest that whenever you have a moment to spare, just find yourself a quiet spot with a comfortable chair, then close your eyes and let your thoughts stray back to days gone by.

When your mind rambles "Down Memory Lane", it is fairly certain that it will eventually dwell upon some of the old shops and businesses from the past, places which you may have frequented regularly in the pursuit of running errands for dear old Mum, or perhaps where you and your ever-loving bought your first roll of lino when you set up home.

In the following pages I shall endeavour to remind you about some of the commercial establishments that flourished in the Portsmouth of yesteryear, but I must emphasize from the start that it will only be the tip of the iceberg, for a dozen books would hardly suffice to do justice to such a vast subject. However, never having been one to turn down a challenge, I have charged into the subject with typewriter ribbons twirling, and I sincerely hope that readers will gain some measure of enjoyment from the ensuing shopping expedition around old Portsmouth and Southsea.

We have a lot of pavement space to cover, many shop windows to gaze in, and plenty of store doors to enter, so I would suggest that you grab your shopping basket and we will be on our way. Oh, and before you step outside your front door into the past, let me give you a couple of tips. As you cross over roads and streets, please be careful not to step into that strange substance that adorns most of the thoroughfares, it is a reminder that horses ruled the roads in those days rather than the belching metallic monsters that we are used to today. And as we enter shops please try not to look too surprised when smiling gents in natty togs leap forward with the greeting: "Good morning, can I be of assistance?." It was the done thing in those times! Finally, please make sure that you have plenty of old money in your purses and wallets, for you never know, you might be able to pick up a bargain!

W. PINK & SONS, LTD
Road.

You & I
By & Bye
Shopping
in Charlotte Street

A Cry from the Streets

Shop proprietors are apt to complain about overheads crippling their trade, the chief of these being taxes, wages, lighting and heating. On the other hand, their counterparts on the market stalls appear to enjoy their trading with less restrictions, their main hazard in carrying out their business in the open-air being the weather, for customers are not likely to linger around very long when the elements are doing their worst.

If the customers are not coming to you, then the sensible thing would seem to be to go to the customers, hence the large number of street vendors that graced our highways and byways in days gone by. Looking back, there always appeared to be more life in our streets then, attributable mainly to those colourful old characters who went about their business complete with horse and cart. Those patient old horses were marvellous, especially those pulling milk, bread, or coal vans or carts. Without prompting they would amble from one house to the next, knowing the round better than their master. Try to teach an electric or motor van to do that!

Like myself, I expect many readers will remember the muffin man, in fact I shall never forget the sight and sound of him standing on the corner and ringing his handbell for all he was worth; within seconds he would be surrounded by eager hands offering copper coins for his wares. Oh, what I would give to be able to go back to those days of youth and re-live the Sunday teatimes of long ago, hot muffins thickly spread with strawberry jam! Cor, sheer ecstasy!

When did you last see a rag and bone man? In our street he was affectionately known as "Old Clo", for when he called out "Old Clothes", he never sounded the last part. Another cry from the streets was "Rag–Muff", rendered in a unique nasal twang it heralded the arrival of a cloth capped gent pushing a barrow, or perhaps sitting atop a cart pulled by a moth-eaten old nag that gave the impression that it was but a few short clip-clops away from its last journey, the glue factory! These Steptoe-type gents could be heard haggling with housewives over the price they would pay them for rabbit skins, the deal usually concluding with the rag and bone man shrugging his shoulders and proclaiming: "Be fair Lady, you have had your meat and bone, I'll give you tuppence for the skin." Rag and bone men now parade under the banner of scrap merchants, drive around in vans, and stick printed leaflets through your letterbox, a far cry from the old days.

During the last century, mat or chair menders used to work the streets, and folk would stagger out with their broken chairs for repair, usually the cane seat portion had caved-in to form a hole, and this could prove rather embarrassing whenever Auntie Lil came around for a cup of tea, for it always took about six of us kids to lift her off the floor. Anyway, the cry of the chairmender proved that he had a sense of humour, it went: "Old chairs to mend, old chairs to mend. If I had as much money as I could spend, I would leave off crying, old chairs to mend".

The Okey Pokey Man was always a welcome figure, for the uninitiated I must explain that this was the old name for ice-cream vendors. Their cry was "Okey Pokey, Penny a Lump, Who will Buy"? This gradually changed over the years to "Icey Picey, Ever so Nicey. They're Loverly" and eventually to the better known "Stop me and Buy One". And we must not forget the travelling knife-grinder, I am pleased to say that we still have a small band of these hard-working chaps in the area, but, unfortunately, they no longer render colourful cries such as: "Knives to Grind. Young gents attend my cry, and bring forth all your knives. The Barber's razors I also grind, and bring out your scissors Wives."

Street trading has been a popular attraction in Portsmouth for hundreds of years, one only has to visit Charlotte Street when the market is in progress to realize that the shoppers' enthusiasm to gain a bargain has not diminished. But more about that particular market place later on in this section, for we must first go back to the Portsmouth of nearly eight hundred years ago. The highlight of the street vendors year was the annual Free Mart Fair, an event that attracted traders and buyers from all over the land. The right to hold the Fair was granted in 1194 by Richard I, a monarch of whom readers of blood and thunder may recall had a passion for romping around in Sherwood Forest with Robin Hood and his faithful sidekicks. The Fair was to be held for fifteen days, and was described as "A free mart for all people, natives or foreigners, to enter the Kingdom, be exempt from all tolls, duties, or impositions, not to be arrested for debt, or oppressed in any way". To put it in a nutshell, it was a free-for-all!

The official opening of the Free Mart Fair was signalled by the displaying of the "Hand", this quaint little ceremony being performed at midnight by the Sergeant-at-Mace, the appearance of the gauntleted hand was guaranteed to raise hearty cheers from the assembled spectators. All was well until 1840, for in that year some unscrupulous varlets had the audacity to actually steal the hand and export it to America. This did not however stop the Fair from continuing, the residents of the High Street quickly organizing a whip-round for a new Open Hand.

The Free Mart Fair was of considerable importance to Portsmouth as a mart for the sale of woollen goods, attracting traders not only from this country, but also from France and Holland. There was a wide choice of goods available, cloths from the West Country, ribbons from Coventry, pottery from Staffordshire, and baskets from Normandy.

The Fair progressed steadily through the years, in fact for several hundreds of years, but by the 19th Century things began to turn sour, the number of stalls selling useful articles had dwindled considerably, their places being taken by peep-shows, menageries, and such like entertainments. It gradually deteriorated into a two-week long rave and booze-up, so it is understandable that the respectable residents of Portsmouth did not look very kindly upon the proceedings. The final crunch came in 1847, although the Fair was held that year, a Bill that had Royal assent decreed that it should be the last. However, in the early hours of 10 July 1848 a group of traders attempted to erect a roundabout on the Parade, but they were soon given their marching orders by a gallant band of our "Boys in Blue". Also, shortly before midnight a gang of fellows assembled in the High Street and called out loudly for the "Glove". They did not get the hand they desired, but they did get the long arm of the law after them for creating a disturbance.

The passing of the Free Mart Fair was a great pity, for in its day it not only brought a good measure of prosperity to the old town, but also brought some cheer into the somewhat dismal lives of some of its inhabitants. They certainly needed a little brightness; if anyone has any doubts let them consider a population count that was taken in Portsmouth in 1811, it revealed that there were 1,711 families residing in 1,084 houses. They also found one house in East Street that contained fourteen families comprising a total of 75 persons. The population figures also tell us that in that same year Portsmouth was inhabited by 2,887 males, and 4,216 females! From this we may conclude that the gents were well catered for in many ways.

In the 1800s The Hard at Portsea presented a busy market scene, for it provided the Pompey housewife of those times with an ideal source from which to get her daily food supplies. As soon as dawn heralded a new day, traders could be seen erecting their stalls on the Hard. They had to be early-risers, for many of them were farmers who had sailed down the harbour from Portchester in order to sell their produce, which included eggs, butter, fruit and vegetables.

Everything from Brewer's Tea to Mumby's Apple Juice. A typical Portsmouth corner shop.

Hudson Brothers Grocery Store, Palmerston Road.

Unfortunately, this waterfront market also attracted many undesirables, such as tricksters and beggars. Regarding two of the latter, a miracle was observed in the 1870s. One beggar had a sign around his neck stating "Blind From Birth", whilst the other lay in a heap by the roadside with a sign saying "Cripple From Birth". Suddenly, it began to rain, in fact it fell down in absolute torrents, accompanied by thunder and lightning. The blind man cried: "I've had enough of this", and ran down the road at a fast lick. At this, the cripple jumped to his feet and shouted: "Ere, wait for me, I'm coming too," and ran after his mate like Sebastian Coe! Yes indeed, a true miracle!

Another busy market was held in Commercial Road, supported by a group of traders who took advantage of another grant made by King Richard, which allowed a market to be held thrice weekly. The traders ignored the fact that the Municipal Corporation Act of 1835 had abolished such ancient charter privileges, and chose to set up stalls three times a week in Commercial Road, usually on Tuesdays, Thursdays, and Saturdays. It is interesting to recall that at one time Commercial Road only ran from Lake Road to All Saints Road, the portion from Edinburgh Road was called Lion Gate Road. It now seems even more remarkable that once there really was a large lake at Lake Road, or Lane, and that at the junction of Lake Road and Commercial Road there was a cattle pound. But, I digress, back to the Commercial Road market. It developed into more of a wholesale market for fruit and vegetables, a sort of Covent Garden where the Portsmouth greengrocers would come to buy their daily stock. A multitude of carts and barrows would come and go in the early hours of the morning, in fact it was more like Piccadilly Circus!

This huge mass of traders and vehicles caused quite an uproar for three days of the week, what with the Dockyard workers cycling through on their way to work, and the first morning trams trying to make their way down Commercial Road, it was like hell let loose, and the air between the tram crews and the market traders was decidedly blue at times! It was just as well that the market did not progress too far into the day, for by mid-morning it had been cleared and Commercial Road was allowed to resume to more normal conditions.

We do not have very far to go to the next market, yes, dear old Charlotte Street of course. This market was founded in 1886 on a site that had been previously occupied by the Eden Brewery, it began with only twelve stalls, each stall being allowed 12sq.ft of trading space, but gradually it grew into the outdoor shoppers' paradise that we are familiar with today. Throughout its near one hundred years existence, this market has endeared itself to generations of Pompey folk, for whom memories of pre-war days in Charlotte Street are sure to evoke fond reminiscences.

For those who were unable to experience the delights of this busy little market in those days, I will attempt to recreate some of the atmosphere. It was really like a little bit of Old Bagdad, with closely-grouped stalls lining the narrow street with just about everything that was saleable on show, from foodstuffs to old bicycle wheels. Traders yelled themselves hoarse in order to raise their voices above their fellow stallholders, and produced a line of patter that almost persuaded their customers that they were getting the Crown Jewels rather than a couple of pounds of spuds!

"Here we are lady, a nice tasty piece of haddock for the old man's supper," so cried Peter Arnett, the housewives' favourite fishmonger. And believe me, it really was tasty. At night, Charlotte Street took on an entirely different look and atmosphere, as the hours of daylight faded the scene was illuminated by spluttering jets hung onto the various stalls, conjuring up a fairy wonderland before your very eyes. Saturday nights especially had a unique atmosphere, with crowds of jostling people hanging around the meat stall as late as possible in the hope of picking up a bargain joint for their Sunday dinner when the meat was auctioned off at greatly reduced prices. When we were young, it all seemed so exciting!

Really, it was all about people, for the market abounded with colourful characters that once seen were never forgotten. I just wish that I had enough space to mention more of them, but I am afraid we shall have to be content with just a few names from markets past. Just before the turn of the century there was a particularly colourful gent who haunted the local markets, he sold quack medicines and called himself the "Great Sequah". He actually originated from Gosport, but had travelled extensively, spending several years in the United States. Whilst there he had learnt some of the tricks of the travelling medicine shows. He returned to this country and Portsmouth, where he would strike a pitch in the markets, or sometimes on the corner of Upper Arundel Street. He would then embark upon an inspired sales patter about the wonders of his product that would cure just about everything from gout to backache. He would draw his audiences with the offer of free dentistry, but his ideas on extracting teeth were very basic, and spectators would have had to be in a pretty bad way to take up Sequah's dental services.

Jumping on a few years, some older readers may recall "Happy Jim", a renowned organ grinder who made the streets of Portsmouth decidedly jollier with his happy brand of music. "Happy Jim", his real name was James Sanson, once had the misfortune to have his organ smashed to pulp in a street riot, but such was his fame, a fund was formed to get him a new one, and even King Edward VII made a contribution. To show his thanks, Jim played his new organ for the King and sang "Count Your Blessings", following which His Majesty shook his hand and wished him good luck. Well, "Happy Jim", who lived in Broad Street, did at least survive longer than King Teddy, dying in 1932 at the age of 70, sadly missed by many Pompey folk.

Moving on to more recent times, another chap who was well known in Charlotte Street was Harry Litchfield, who died in 1962. Harry was known by one and all as the "Onion King", trading in the market for over thirty years. He had begun by selling bacon from a stall there, but when stricter regulations controlling the sale of meat were introduced, he turned to onions. Some writers would seize the opportunity to make a terrible pun and remark that Harry "knew his onions", but realizing that all my readers have impeccable taste, I would not dare use such a dreadful pun!

What is that, you are feeling whacked-out with all this fresh air? Not to worry, we shall be moving into the great indoors very shortly, but I do hope that this brief reminder of some of the outdoor markets and street traders of bygone years has helped to whet your appetite for what is to follow. So, if you will kindly follow me, we will now step through the welcoming doors of the Portsmouth Emporium.

"Good Morning, sir and madam, can I help you?" "No thank you, we are only looking, so will you kindly take your hands from off my wallet!"

Ground Floor
Groceries–Bread–Meat–Milk etc.

Did you hear about the assistant on the Co-op meat counter who sat down on the bacon-slicer by mistake, and got a little "behind" in her orders!

I am sorry about that awful joke, but it does help to lead us into the next subject on our shopping list, which you will have no doubt have realized by now concerns food. Food is, of course, one of the main necessities of life, although it does sometimes seem to me that half the people in the world are worried because they cannot get enough of it, whilst the other half seem more concerned that they are getting too much, the spectacular rise of weight-watching clubs confirming this point of view. Many scientists would have us believe that we are in for a drastic change in our eating habits in the future, food as we know it will be a thing of the past, and if you feel hungry all you will have to do is reach for a bottle and help yourself to a steak and kidney pie flavoured pill. Shopping habits could change as well, we may get our weekly shopping in chemists rather than grocers shops!

Mind you, when one thinks of the number of small corner shops that have disappeared in recent years, I sometimes wonder if the pill habit is not already with us. The art of shopkeeping has always had a strong element of dog-eat-dog about it, with little shops falling to small self-service stores, which in turn have been swallowed by supermarkets, and at the present time we seem to be moving into the age of the hypermarket. The reason for this development can be largely attributed to a change in shopping habits that has been brought about by the popularity of the family motor car, for many folk are now in a position to drive into one of the large grocery palaces and get their weekly needs all in one go.

In the old days there was more of a tendency to live from day to day, hence the daily trips to the little shop on the corner. There were two main reasons for this, the first being the lack of money to buy food in bulk, the second being the lack of home refrigeration. Regarding the latter, in those days we had those weird contraptions known as meat safes, although they did not do a great deal to keep food fresh, they did help to keep the flies off to a certain extent. Mind you, without the wonders of modern refrigeration and hygienically-wrapped food, I personally think that the food tasted better in those days, or perhaps they had a tastier breed of fly then!

Regarding the former, a decided advantage with the corner grocer was that he was generally quite happy to put it on the slate until the end of the week, but of course he had to know his customers and have an ability to differentiate between good and honest working folk, and the not-so-honest working folk. Yes, in many ways he had to be a student of life.

Throughout history, shopkeepers have not only had to contend with trying to attract customers into their premises, but they have also been engaged in a never-ending battle with the authorities. Perhaps this was just as well as far as the customers are concerned, for honest dealing was not a strong point with many of the Portsmouth traders of old, a fact highlighted by the October Sessions of 1657 when no less than 34 shopkeepers of the town were brought to court for having weights too light, and measures too little! It was really quite easy to take advantage of the poor old customer, for shops then were very poorly lit, with very little daylight coming through the small-paned windows that were in vogue then.

Rather dingy oil lamps were used for street lighting in the 1700s. but the big breakthrough came in the early 1800s when gas lighting was first introduced in Portsmouth. St George's Square in Portsea was honoured with being the first part of the town to be lit, with much hissing and spluttering commencing in the June of 1821. By 1823 it had spread to Old Portsmouth, and to

Landport by 1825. Improved street lighting brought both good and bad news, the good being that the inhabitants of Portsmouth could go out during the hours of darkness without fear of being mugged by footpads. The bad news was for the poor old shop assistants, the shops were able to stay open later, thus adding to their already long working hours.

Looking on the bright side, better street lighting was a protection against crime to a certain degree. Unfortunately, it came too late to save a much respected grocer named Richard Dart, who in 1800 was found murdered behind the counter of his store in St.James Street, a foul deed that shocked the respectable residents of Southsea. Still thinking of crime, and robbery and break-ins in particular, it is interesting to recall that around this time there was in use a valuable weapon against criminals, the famous Chubb Lock. Not many people realize that Mr. Chubb invented his lock whilst living in Portsmouth, his idea originating from Daniel Street.

You can see how easy it is to wander, locks really come under the hardware department, so we had better return to the grocery counter. Donning my white apron I will now provide a brief reminder of some of the provision stores in Portsmouth past, and who better to begin with than Pink's, a name renowned not only in the world of commerce, but also in the expansion of our great city. This grocery empire began with one man, William Pink, who was born near Bishop's Waltham in 1830. On leaving school he served an apprenticeship with a Winchester grocer, then as soon as he was old enough he went to London to work in the trade. After gaining valuable experience, he came to Portsmouth to manage Earl's Grocery Store at 112, Commercial Road. A few years later he returned to London to take up a post as manager for the Parisian Chocolate Company, a firm that had been founded by several French noblemen after they had fled to London during the French Revolution. But, William's first love was the grocery trade, and he went to work for Fortnum & Mason, one of the most renowned grocery emporiums in the world.

After gaining more experience, and a respectable bank balance, William Pink returned to Portsmouth to buy out Earl's, the store that he had previously managed. And so, William was established in his own business at the ripe old age of 28. At that time there were only five or six other grocery shops in the area, but he had what could be described as a prime site. On one side he had John Hicks stonemason's yard, and on the other side was a second hand tool dealer. By working 17 hours a day, William was soon in a position to expand his premises and take over the stonemason's yard, and the tool store, which by that time was known as Smith's Eating House. The grocery business gained such a reputation, that the corner of Surrey Street and Commercial Road became known as Pink's Corner. It is interesting to note that in earlier times this corner spot was where all the chimney sweeps of Portsmouth would assemble on May Day to hold their annual festival, an excuse for much dancing and jollification.

In 1887 the shop fascia proclaimed "William Pink & Sons", announcing that his three sons, Ernest, Harold, and Victor had entered the business. At one time the family actually lived over the Commercial Road premises, and Sir Harold Pink, as he became later, was born in a room that in later years was to become his office. Harold was to serve several terms as Mayor of Portsmouth, but he was really only following in his father's footsteps, for William Pink had entered the council in 1866, and became Mayor ten years later. One of his proudest moments was when he was rewarded for his good works by being knighted by Queen Victoria in 1891.

Sir William Pink, grocer extraordinary, died in 1906, leaving his sons to carry on the family name in business and in public affairs. This they did with great gusto, opening branches at an alarming rate, in 1914 Pink's had 12 shops employing 314 staff, by

Co-op laundry service.

It also pays to advertise.

'Gotta Lotta Bottle', milkcarts, 1930s.

Copnor Co-op Dairy, 1929.

Co-op in Fratton Road, destroyed by fire in 1934.

1920 they had 25 shops with 507 staff, and when they became a limited company in 1933 they could boast a total of 44 branches employing 700 people. Sir William's great-grandson, Ralph Bonner-Pink, joined the business in 1930, and became a director with a special responsibility for advertising. By this time Pink's were so well known I should hardly think they had need to advertise, for they were an institution.

During the war when the air raids over Portsmouth were at their worst in 1940–41, food shops were high on the list of places to protect, even the little corner shops, for just one incendiary bomb could put at risk food supplies for hundreds of people. You can imagine the feelings when it was learnt that Pink's warehouse in St. George's Square was ablaze, but alas, emergency services arrived too late to save the building, and a great quantity of much-needed food was destroyed. Pink's corner shop in Commercial Road also took a battering during that raid, but mostly from looters, for in the cold light of day it was found that boxes of wines and tobacco had disappeared overnight, no doubt bound for the black market. After the war this once great grocery empire began to dwindle, shops were closed until you could count the number of branches on one hand. How could this possibly happen to a business that was once so powerful? I am afraid Pink's were one of the early victims of the supermarket war.

I expect several readers will still remember Pink's famous Tarragona Wine, one glass per day was guaranteed to kill all known germs. They were also well known for their many brands of tea, and when we contemplate the wonders of this nectar we must spare a thought for a formidable son of Portsmouth, James Hanway. Hanway was born in Portsmouth in 1712, at that moment in time nobody would have had the slightest idea that he would become one of the world's most outstanding philanthropists. After enjoying early success in business, James went on to found the Marine Society, the Magdalen Hospital in London, countless Sunday Schools, and to become the first man in England to use an umbrella in public, amongst many other things. He also wrote and published several books, using them to announce his hatred of many things, including those of the Jewish following. But there was something that he hated even worse than this, what he described as the baneful habit of tea-drinking. For many years James Hanway campaigned against the evils of tea, proclaiming his opinion that the many ills from which the nation was suffering at that time were due to the effects of this vile brew. Two hundred years on, I am sure that firms such as Ford's would agree with Hanway's views, the effects of tea-breaks have certainly taken their toll on the nation!

The Co-operative history of trading is so vast and various, it has been difficult to decide which floor of this book to put them on, for they are equally at home in the furnishing, drapery, and hardware departments. But, as their trading began with the provision of food, it is in this that I will include them.

Officially, the Co-operative movement began in Rochdale in 1840, but Portsmouth could claim that it started here some 44 years prior. This came about when the Dockyard men met to found the Union Society, an organization formed with a view to building a mill that would put the price of bread within the reach of the poorer classes. So, this venture of 1796 could have been the first Co-op in the land, but don't tell the people of Rochdale that!

The Co-operative movement began in earnest in Portsmouth in 1873, fifteen dedicated chaps banded together to commence the Portsea Island Mutual Co-operative Society, which I shall refer to hereafter as PIMCO. To say that it had a modest beginning would be an understatement, for the small shop that they rented in Charles Street could only be opened for business after working hours on Friday and Saturday nights, with the intrepid 15 taking it in turns to don white aprons and play the role of grocery assistants. The door of the shop was opened for business on the evening of

May 9, and when it was locked up for the night the enthusiastic group of part-timers found that they had amassed the magnificent sum of nine quid in the "Jack-and-Jill". Or to the uninitiated, the till. Without the aid of refrigeration they were unable to store perishable foods such as the three B's, bread, butter, and bacon, so at the close on Saturday nights the workers had to buy the surplus themselves!

Co-operativism, that must be a new word that I have just invented, really caught on in Portsmouth, and very soon a move was made to larger premises in nearby Besant Road. Within ten years of their formation they were in a position to open the first branch shop in Kingston Road, it was of course to be the first of many. By maintaining a fairly steady dividend at I/6d. in the £, the expansion was tremendous, by 1910 PIMCO had a membership of 9,140 served by 17 grocery shops, but by leaping on another 25 years we find that by 1935 the membership had jumped terrifically to 45,500, with 42 grocery stores in the Portsmouth area, in addition to 16 butchery shops.

Despite protests from local dairy concerns, PIMCO entered the dairy business in 1913 with a depot in Fratton Grove, moving operations later to Copnor Road. History has shown that the private dairy people had good cause to worry over the Co-op entry into the milk game, for many of them disappeared off the map never to be heard of again, but the Co-op has expanded to cover a large area, and has a huge depot at Drayton. One thing is for sure, we have to pay a heck of a lot more for our daily pinta now. I do not wish to upset readers too much, but I simply must put on record that the price of that first bottle of Co-op milk in 1913 was a penny-halfpenny a pint!

The year 1928 saw the establishment of PIMCO's first hairdressing salon in Albert Road, and the following year was notable for the commencement of their butchery department. Then in 1930 the society's magnificent drapery building was opened in Fratton Road, and one may presume that its opening came as quite a big blow to some of the large stores in Landport and Southsea that had previously dominated the drapery and fashion scene. In 1933, the Central Grocery Department was transferred to a modern store in Fratton Road, thus making Fratton an important shopping centre. But, disaster was not far away, for in the July of 1934 the society's central premises ar Fratton was ravaged by a terrible fire. After they had got over the initial shock, the staff displayed a tremendous show of loyalty and got on with the task of getting back into business as soon as possible.

The PIMCO did their bit for the war effort by carrying on through the hostilities, then after the war they surged on with forward thinking to open Britain's first self-service shop in 1948. That event is well remembered by Basil Tucker, the society's publicity manager, for he had to write by hand all the notices and hanging signs for the opening. Basil retired in 1982 after 34 years service, during that time the PIMCO annual turnover increased from £3½ million to £100 million. As I have always said, it pays to advertise.

Bringing the Co-op story up to date, in keeping with modern trends many branch shops have closed in the last decade, but a huge hypermarket was built near the motorway link at Havant, and has enjoyed tremendous success since opening. In the outlying areas, PIMCO has taken over a large supermarket at Brockhurst in Gosport in 1983, this had previously been run by Price-rite, International, and Mainstop, in that order. By adding the Co-op initials to those of the three previous owners, readers may be amazed to discover that they produce the title 'PIMCO'.

Looking back to the middle of the last century, it would appear that the food-lovers of Portsmouth were well catered for, the White's Directory for 1859 listing no fewer than 185 grocers. As the population expanded, so did the number of grocers, and we find that the Portsea Island of the 1920's could boast at least 270.

Franklin, the Southsea baker.

Brunton's for bread.

The Portsmouth Dairy.

'Stop me and buy one'.

Bishop's Grocery Store, St. Mary's Road.

Brooklands Dairy.

Pink's North End branch, 1905.

Father Dolling of St. Agatha's, with Lipton Boys, 1896.

The latter included many well-known chain store names, many of which had several branches in Portsmouth. I am sure that most readers will remember the Maypole Dairy, Peark's, Lipton's, Home & Colonial, World's Stores, International Tea Company, and David Greig's. If pushed to provide the names of a couple of smaller grocers, I would probaby choose Banks Brothers of North End, and Brewer's in Marmion Road. I am pleased to say that the name of Banks has been maintained on the corner of Gladys and North End avenues, namely Douglas Banks & Son. Ltd. And of course Edwin Brewer's renowned tea and coffee blending establishment is still going strong, I could stand outside sniffing in that delicious aroma all day long.

As a parting shot about grocers, I will remind older readers, and astound younger readers, with a few grocery prices from the early part of this century. A dozen eggs would set you back 1/2d., and for the same sum you could buy a pound of butter. It cost 2d. for 4lb. of potatoes, 1d. or 2d. for a pound of apples, and tuppence for a pound of sugar. In a blue bag of course! Well, I did warn you to bring some old money along with you!

A Slice of Life.

Thinking back to when I was but a mere nipper, I recall that I was one of the fattest boys in the school, a factor not helped by a schoolboy passion for thick slices of crusty bread spread lavishly with jam. Sweets never bothered me all that much, I preferred the stodgy things of life. Whenever I had managed to save a copper or two I would rush into a baker's shop after school and ask for a pennyworth of stale cakes. I think the genial lady behind the counter must have taken a shine to my cherubic features, for I generally rolled out of the shop with a bag bulging with cakes, and I must say they certainly never tasted stale to me. I wonder what Bakers would say now if kids went in and asked for a pennyworth of stale cakes?

Like our grocery friends, the bakers of Portsmouth also had frequent skirmishes with the authorities over the years. One of the earliest clashes that I have on record took place in 1569, with the town's rulers coming on strong and issuing an order to the bakers that "no manner of baker within this town should bake or sell any kind of bread other than which shall be sweet and holesom for man's body, and that it should be of just measure". But it was the turn of the bakers to lay down the law in 1660, for they were not happy with the way that they were treated in their dealings with the Navy, and issued a statement to the effect that they refused to supply any more bread to the King's ships unless their outstanding debts were paid immediately.

But the biggest rumpus occurred in 1800, for in the January of that year the bakers of Portsmouth went on strike. They wanted to raise the price of their bread, but it was controlled by the Mayor and the Borough Magistrates. Eventually, the Mayor and his gang gave in, and bread prices increased. And that is when the trouble really started, towards the end of the year the town's residents were complaining bitterly about bread prices skyrocketing. Events took a nasty turn, and even spread to Southampton, where the cavalry had to be called out to protect the bakers. In Portsmouth an angry crowd assembled in the Old Rope Walk and in St.George's Square, set on destruction. Thanks to the intervention of the Mayor, Mr.Goldson, peace was soon restored. This was hardly surprising, for the Mayor had the backing of a small army, comprising over 100 special constables that he had rapidly sworn in. The price war had been brought about by a poor harvest, but I am pleased to say that the following harvest was excellent and the price of bread was reduced from 3/5d. a gallon to 1/6d.

In years gone by, once the bakers had gone to the trouble of heating their ovens, they made sure that they did not waste that heat by operating a kind of "Bake-away, Take-away" service. For a few coppers Pompey folk could have their dinners cooked in the bakers' ovens, and on Sundays they would generally drop their dinners off on the way to church, then collect them ready-cooked on the way home, this was a popular practice in the Portsmouth of the last century, despite an unfortunate incident that happened at Mr. Davey's bakehouse in Charlotte Row in 1810. A man pretending to have his dinner baked there actually stole a dish belonging to another man, it contained a shoulder of mutton, pudding, and potatoes. Because the food belonged to a family man of poor circumstance, the robbery was indeed a dastardly act.

Have you ever wondered about the origin of your name? In earlier times abandoned children were giving strange names, usually associated with the place where they were found, hence John Portsmouth, or Mary London. This was not a bad practice really, unless you were unlucky enough to have been abandoned in Scunthorpe, for Fred Scunthorpe is hardly the sort of name you see emblazoned in lights outside a West End theatre. At this point I will probably cast doubts in the minds of anybody named Baker, or perhaps Butcher, this is not intentional I assure you, but it is true that in times gone by if an infant was found abandoned on the doorstep of a baker's shop, it was likely that it would be annointed with the name of Baker.

The above was the fate of a well known Pompey character named Billy Baker, and when he grew older he would earn a few coppers by delivering newspapers or running errands for anyone who took pity on him, this enabled him to purchase a night's kip in the Tower Lane dosshouse at Point, otherwise it was a case of sleeping rough for the night in Piper's Alley. Although Billy Baker had an association with bakers through his adopted name, he could also be connected with shoemaking, for he was one of the last pupils of the renowned John Pounds. But more about that particular gentleman later.

When perusing old directories, it will be found that bakers are very often linked with confectioners and pastrycooks, and William Kimbell was a craftsman who could claim success in all three trades. Born in Chichester in 1880, William left school at thirteen to join his father in the bakery business, then at 17 he went to London to study catering and confectionery. He returned to the area to open shops in Chichester, Bognor, and Tunbridge Wells before finally settling in Portsmouth, where incidentally he got married at Milton Church in 1904. He took over the old established firm of William Butler in Southsea, then expanded rapidly by purchasing other shops in the vicinity. He was ever-striving to perfect his confectionery, and in doing so he won some of the highest awards in England for his decoration skills. In the 1920s he was asked to carry out the catering for functions at the Guildhall, a symbol that he had really arrived, for it was a much sought-after position. One of his finest creations was the decorating of a table for the visit of the Prince of Wales in 1926, this was the occasion when the Prince was presented with the Freedom of the City. The business was formed into a company in 1935, and was known as W.Kimbell & Son. Although William had retired in 1938, he returned to look after the business when his son Laurie was called into the forces for World War Two. After the war William continued his retirement at his home on Portsdown Hill, and concentrated on tending his beloved chrysanthemums until he died in 1959. I expect many readers will have fond memories of partaking of a pot-of-tea for two at Kimbells's in Osborne Road, or perhaps in one of their other establishments in the city. I am pleased to say that Kimbell's is still in business in Osborne Road, providing banqueting facilities.

Referring to the war a few lines back, the problem of food rationing was something many of us had to cope with. The last war may be fairly fresh in our minds, but the shortage of bread was something that featured very strongly in the First World War also. Bread was rationed to the extent of four pounds per head weekly, but towards the end of the war it was governed more by price, for

Co-op transport 1930s, old next to new.

Co-op Copnor branch, 1912.

the cost of food had increased almost 100 per cent from the start of hostilities in 1914. It is interesting to recall that tradesmen were urgently required for war service in 1915, and posters were displayed around Portsmouth appealing for butchers and bakers to enlist in the Army Service Corps, all they had to do was pop down to the recruiting office in Commercial Road and sign on the dotted line.

For those who had a passion for dainty cakes and delicious pastries, the place to go was Brunton's in Palmerston Road, or perhaps their Victoria Road South branch. If you could not wait until you got home to sample their confectionery delights, Brunton's also had an excellent restaurant where one could scoff in comfort. Let me remind you of a few bakery names from Portsmouth past, I am afraid I only have room for some of the big boys, mostly concerns that had more than one shop. The big three comprised Smith & Vosper, Batchelor & Putman, and Ward's New Road Bakery, with branches well into double figures. Then we had Price Brothers, Sam Knight, Arthur Millard, Harry Dike, and of course Campion's. A solo shop that I would like to mention is the Premier Bakery of R.A.Scott in Devonshire Avenue, which I am pleased to say is still selling bread. When I pass Scott's shop I cannot resist looking at the old metal display signs over the fascia, a reminder of the past to be sure. Add to the above names those of William Pink and the Co-op, two other popular concerns who sold bread, and that gives us at least a dozen bakers who have "given unto us our daily bread", but of course there were hundreds more over the years.

And that is where we must bid farewell to the subject of bread and bakers, needless to say, we shall never be able to buy a cottage loaf for tuppence three farthings again!

Tea Break

At this stage, we have made such good progress around the Portsmouth Emporium, I think a tea break would be in order. Most of the larger departmental stores could boast flourishing restaurants, as we shall discover later on. But for now, let us think back to some of the names that made a living from serving cups of tea and tasty dishes.

For sheer nostalgic delight, I cannot do better than to start with the celebrated "Swiss Cafe & Restaurant", and the name that we associate with this revered eating place is that of Albertolli. Two Swiss brothers, Baptiste and Bartholomew Albertolli, came to Portsmouth in 1893 and opened a cafe in Commercial Road. They did well, and Baptiste left later to open the "Swiss Cafe & Restaurant" on the site that most readers will be familiar with, the Arcade and Edinburgh Road. Before long the Albertolli empire had also spread to the Isle of Wight, catering for hungry trippers at Union Street in Ryde. It really was a family business, Baptiste was married to Louisa, and they produced their own little army of waiters and washer-uppers, five sons and six daughters. There is hardly any need for me to add that the Albertolli's were staunch Roman Catholics! Baptiste died in 1936 at the age of 71, leaving his family to carry on the business. Perhaps it was just as well, for he was spared from the awful sight of the Commercial Road that he knew so well being destroyed a few years later in 1941. His brother, Bart Albertolli, ran his Continental Cafe, Restaurant & Lobster Bar in Commercial Road with his own family for many years, until he died in 1950. Baptiste's wife Louisa died the same year, and I am afraid that the Swiss Cafe itself died along with the Arcade in 1958. Yes, gone, but certainly not forgotten.

One fine day in 1920 there was a good deal of excitement in Commercial Road, over 700 people attended the opening of the Corner House Restaurant on the corner of Swan Street. It was indeed a most magnificent and ornate building, occupying three floors, with a Grand Grill Room on the ground floor, the Victory Hall on the next floor, and a cafe on the top floor. The proprietor was Charles Brown, a well known councillor, and the construction of the building was in the able hands of another esteemed Portsmouth councillor, Frank Privett. It was the absolute epitomy of luxury and comfort, with music for eating-by provided by a London orchestra, and the chef had previously exercised his culinary arts at the Cafe Royale in London. The Corner House Restaurant was taken over in later years by Kimbell's, and continued after the war. Alas, this once resplendent building no longer resounds to the clash of knives and forks doing battle to the strains of orchestral music, but if one stands in front of the Theatre Royal and looks across to the Swan Street corner, turning your gaze upwards you will see a faded reminder of the glory that was once the Corner House Restaurant.

Palmerston Road was a favourite spot in the old days for shoppers to have a welcome tea break, they certainly had a wide choice of establishments, including the Mikado Cafe, the aforementioned Brunton's, and the Cafe Royal. The latter offered the choicest wines, cigars, and cigarettes with the food, and an orchestra played nightly from 7–9.30 p.m. A luncheon there would set you back 2/6d., and if you returned for the evening rave-up a dinner would cost you 4/6d. The Mikado was also a popular venue for dancing, and the Tango was the most requested dance, but not really recommended to those who had just eaten a great meal.

Mr. J. Madden was the proprietor of the "Handyman Restaurant" in Unicorn Road, and "Madden's Restaurant and Hotel" in Station Road. Both of these Landport establishments were highly popular with Jack Tar, for he could always be sure of a welcome cup of char or a clean bed for the night at a reasonable price. The sailor of yesterday was not all that fussy about his food, it was a case of quantity rather than quality, for those who preferred the latter the place to go was Horne's Restaurant in Commercial Road, for they proclaimed that they only catered for the lady or gentleman with an educated palate.

Whilst in Commercial Road, we might pop into Lyons Restaurant at No.164. I must admit that old Joe Lyons eating houses were my favourite haunts in days gone by; they were sort of nice places to take nice girls. I won't divulge where I took bad girls! Anyway, Lyons in Commercial Road was erected on the site of what had previously been the famous Bakers Arms public house, a drinking den that was demolished in 1914. There is an interesting story concerning the Bakers Arms, in earlier times the proprietor Mr. Pitt brought charges against the Minister of Lake Road Baptist Chapel, the Rev. Charles Joseph. Pitt claimed the Minister had slandered his pub badly in a sermon, the charge was proved and Mr. Joseph was ordered to pay a fine and costs of £200. He refused to pay and faced prison, but he was saved by his flock of Lake Road Baptists who managed to raise the money required.

Careful Brown, you will be on to pubs before you know where you are, back to cafes and restaurants. As a final fling on the subject I will throw readers just a few more names. In King's Road there was the King's Restaurant, run by Mr. Pini, or perhaps you preferred Beti's Cafe in the same road. In Russell Street there was Mr. Ferrari's Russell Cafe, and not too far away there was the Ruby Cafe run by Mrs Zazzi. Have you noticed that most of them were run by people with foreign names, I think we had better finish on a British note, how about Smith? Yes, Smith's Hotel & Restaurant in Castle Road, Southsea.

Some of you may have smoked a cigarette whilst partaking of this tea or coffee break, don't worry, I do not intend to start listing tobacconists shops, but I wonder if many readers can remember the rather unusual sales gimmick that was on display outside the tobacconists store of Collis's in Commercial Road. This took the form of an old figurehead from a wooden battleship, depicting a Scottish Highlander. I believe it disappeared around 1925 from outside the shop, and wonder if it still exists somewhere in the area?

Mr. Moore's Butchers Shop in Somers Road, 1909.

Right, tea break over, we must be on our way. We are still dealing with foodstuff, so we are still on the ground floor of the Emporium.

A Chop off of the Old Block

I have always felt that those who take up the butchery or fishmongery trade have to be of a special breed, and exceptionally tough, for through necessity they have to work in very cold conditions, unheated premises that are very often completely open at the front and devoid of any window protection. In addition to this, the produce that they handle is cold and wet. No, neither profession would suit me!

Another facet of the meat and fish trade is that they have to use sharp tools, such as knives or cleavers. I must admit that keen edges make me nervous, a fear that began many years ago when

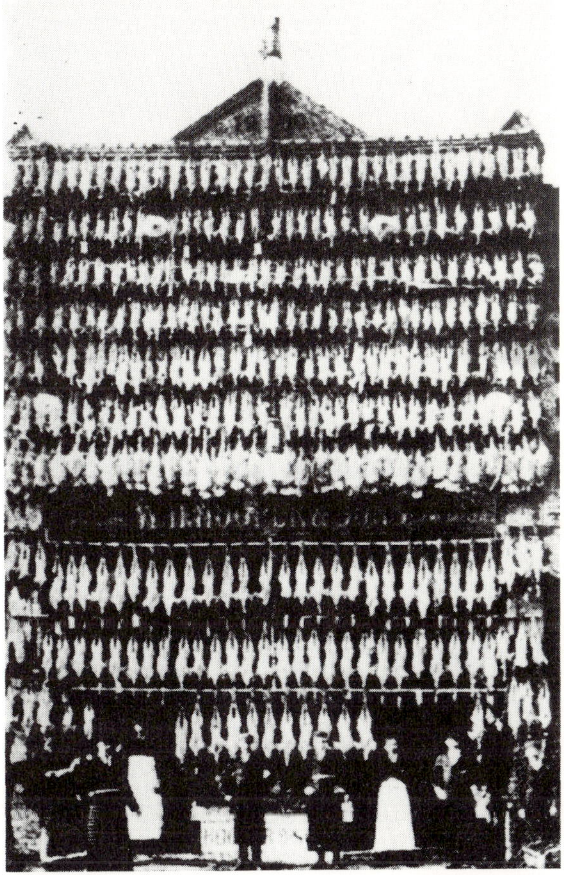

Xmas display in Great Southsea Street, at least 340 birds on show.

Maynards Sweetshop in Grove Road South.

an old-timer persuaded me that I would get a closer shave if I used an open type cut-throat razor. I never could stand the sight of blood, especially if it is mine! So imagine how poor old George Few felt in 1929, he was serving behind the counter of his butchers shop when a lady came in and ordered a piece of meat. George prepared the order with his back to the counter, when he turned around to his horror he found that the customer had picked up one of his knives and calmly slit her throat! Urgh! Strangely enough, a few years prior to this incident there was a case in which a well known Arundel Street butcher, who was also a respected councillor, committed suicide by stabbing himself in the throat with one of the instruments of his trade.

This is all getting a bit macabre, so let us get away from the subject of knives. How about guns? Many butchers in the old days kept shotguns as part of their equipment, generally for slaughter purposes. It may seem strange now, but the police very often enlisted the help of butchers if they needed arms. In one unfortunate incident, a horse was waiting with a cart attached outside the Police Station in Albert Road. Suddenly, a kiddies balloon burst in the street, making a great bang and causing the horse to bolt. The frightened animal hurtled down Albert Road at a furious pace, but when it drew near to the Salvation Army Citadel the cart swayed and crashed into a stationary van, the horse shot straight out of the shafts and hit the road with tremendous force, breaking both it's forelegs. A policeman ran into the nearest butchers shop, which happened to belong to Charlie Horn, and Charles went to the scene immediately with his gun and put the poor ceature out of its misery. That happened in 1928, and with motors replacing horses on our roads this kind of incident could hardly happen today, although I would suspect that when their cars break down, some motorists would be sorely tempted to shoot a couple of rounds into their vehicle if they had the means!

Meat has always been a desirable part of our diet, but unfortunately it was not always in everyone's reach in days gone by. Many poor folk in Edwardian times were glad to live on fagot stew, or giblet stew, they made a cheap meal if you were on the breadline. Some people thought they would be better off in the workhouse, and perhaps they would have been. In 1837 new regulations were introduced for the diet of inmates in the Portsmouth Workhouse, this allowed time to partake of a warm dinner with meat every day of the week. Prior to this it had been the practice to have five bread and cheese days in the fortnight. A rebellion almost took place in the workhouse in 1872, the authorities decreed that the Governor and Matron should have their daily ration of meat reduced from 5 lbs. to 2 lbs! It is interesting to note that the children of the officers of the workhouse were allowed one pint of ale per day.

In the mid 1800s the choristers of St. Thomas's always went to choir practice earlier than they need have done, the great attraction being the old coaching table that was adjacent to the church. One part of it was used by a blacksmith, but the other part was used by a local pork butcher for killing pigs. The boys would look on in awe as the butcher held the squealing pigs down on a trestle and slit their throats, then the warm carcases were scalded, scraped, and prepared for a quick sale.

Butchers and fishmongers, akin to other traders, did not escape the beady eyes of the authorities. In 1717 the Borough constables were urged to frequent market places in search of poor quality meat or undersized fish. With fish, a guide was issued to aid the watchdogs. Measured from the eyes of the fish to the tail they had to measure no less than sixteen inches in the case of turbot, six inches for whiting, eight for sole, and twelve inches for cod, bass, or mullet.

Although butchers are in a trade that calls for the slaughter of animals, in days of old they took great pride in possessing fine horses for their stables. One of this number was a Mr. Hall, a respected Charlotte Row butcher in the early 1800s. He made a wager for £10 a side with Mr. Upsdale of Hambledon that he could walk or ride his favourite horses from the Market House in Portsmouth to the Elephant & Castle in London in under twelve hours. The indefatigable Mr. Hall won the bet, completing the journey in 10 hours and 55 minutes.

Although there is nobody left who could remember Mr. Hall, some older readers may recall Highbury Street butcher Harry Marchment. Born in 1861, Harry left the Bell School at 14 to work in the butchers shop of Mr. William Smith, then in 1881 he started up in business on his own account from a small shop in Brunswick Street. From this small beginning a mammoth meat organization was to develop, and at the time of the 1897 Diamond Jubilee Fleet Review Harry was supplying meat to the warships of nine nations. He was well thought of in butchery circles and served as President of the Portsmouth & District Master Butchers and Cattle Dealers Association. When Harry Marchment died he left £36,000 in his will, a tidy sum for 1929.

Butcher Fred Currey also died in 1929, he had opened his first shop in 1889 at the age of nineteen. Before long he had three shops around Portsmouth, specialized in pig breeding in this country, and helped to fight off the importation of bacon from the Continent. Fratton butcher William Billing was also a past President of the Master Butchers Association, but he will chiefly be remembered for his role as Lord Mayor of Portsmouth for the 1932–33 term. In more recent times, many folk who lived in the Milton Road area will have fond memories of Harry Smith. Harry started his own butchers shop in 1936, and carried on until 1973, when he retired at the age of 79.

Naming Portsmouth butchers could seemingly go on and on, well into the hundreds. We shall have to make do with a few of the big boys, so here we go. G.A. Cooper, Dewhurst's, Eastmans, W.& R. Fletcher, George Harris, Albert Durant, James Gale, A. T. Hart, Charles Saunders, George Ware, J. Watkins, Wickens & Co., Tom and Frank Westbrook, Percy Lloyd – Stop! I must have room for a few fishmongers!

I must confess that I am not awfully fond of the smell of fish, for me it is bad enough in the house, let alone fishmongers shops. Perhaps it was just as well that it was sold in the open in earlier times, gents such as Mr. Curtis would ride around old Pompey on their fishcarts, generally pulled by a patient old donkey. But when we start thinking about fishmongery names from the past, I am sure that the aforementioned Peter Arnett of Charlotte Street fame is the name that most readers will think of. But there are of course a few other names to add, the name of Slape for one, with shops run by Charles, Sydney, Tom, Bert, Harry, Fred and Arthur Slape. Then we have Sibley, Hooper's, Jennings, Owens, Pullen, Patterson, and Barnett to complete the list.

There is one thing that I am certain about, Christmas has never been the same for me since butchers and poulterers stopped hanging their produce outside their shops at holiday times, sometimes stacked to the very highest point of the building. Many of the shopkeepers had so many birds hung up outside it would take them all night to take them down, so they employed nightwatchmen to keep an eye on the goods. Just imagine this practice being carried out now, the birds would be as black as Newgate's Knocker within minutes from car exhaust fumes!

They Drove the Fastest Milkcarts in the South

For our last food topic, milk and dairies, I was in a quandary whether or not to include it in the "Cry From the Streets" section, for it really is an outdoor occupation. On the other hand, bottles of milk were also sold from shops, usually when visitors arrived unexpectedly and you were short of it to make a cup of tea. In line with Common Market policy, it could be that in the future we will have to get our milk from shops, prices will be more competitive,

Southsea's oldest milkman, c.1914. Always a good for a "yoke".

so a personal delivery service to the doorstep will not be economically viable. Personally, I hope this will never come about, I like to hear the friendly whistling of a milkman first thing in the morning coming down my front path.

Perhaps I am a little biased, for my old Dad was a milkman in days gone by, as were several other members of the family. Of course that was in the horse-drawn milk cart days, and I looked forward to helping Dad on the round on Saturdays, for I could sit atop the milk cart with the reins in my hands pretending that I was Buffalo Bill being chased by Indians. Kitty, the milk horse, never appeared to take a great deal of interest in my Wild West meanderings, she was more content to chew the top off someone's hedge.

One thing from my youth I do remember quite vividly, is that I never saw much of Dad in those days, for he was always out at the crack of dawn and never got home until about half-past six in the evening. He was even later when there was ice and snow about, and once the poor old horse had slipped down, it was a heck of a job to get it up again, But of course, electric floats and handcarts solved that sort of caper.

In the old days milk was delivered twice daily. Customers had their own personal cans which they hung outside the front of the house, when the milkman arrived he would ladle milk into the can from a copper churn. Most of the cans had lids, which explains why sparrows then flew around with bent beaks, the coming of the soft foil bottle top must have been a blessing for them. Like other traders, dairies also had problems with weights and measures inspectors, who frequently made unexpected checks for quantity and quality of the milk that they sold. Whilst publicans in the past were regularly accused of watering down their beer, dairies also suffered with similar charges made against them regarding milk. Unfortunately, in the majority of cases the authorities were on the side of right with their accusations, and the dairyman would have

'Pot of tea for two, please'.

Established in 1896. Own brand of 'Novic' cigarettes cost 7/11d. for 100.

The Guildhall, made in cake.

to pay a fine. But I am afraid they never learnt their lesson, for the same dairies came before the magistrates time and time again.

Comparing old and new methods of milk provision, the chief difference would seem to be that nowadays we have fewer dairies, but they are much larger concerns. In the old days there were absolutely scores of dairies, but they were mostly small businesses. Back in the last century the name that dominated the dairy world in Portsmouth was that of Pharoah, covering Portsea Island with milk rounds run by James, John, Joseph, Martha, Richard, and Thomas Pharoah. The opposition included dairymen and cowkeepers such as Tom Marshall, Joe Lampard, John Cole, Henry Eyles, Edwin Boulton, Henry House, James Humby, Sam Brazill, Tom Knott, Joe Abrahams, and Francis Lenkoske. To name a few.

Moving into this century, I am sure that many readers will be familiar with the name of Gauntlett and Walker Dairies. This combination came about in 1958 when James Archibald Walker became equal partner with Victor Gauntlett, it was the marriage of two of the oldest established dairy businesses in the area. "Arch" Walker was the third generation of a family dairy that was established in the 1790s, it moved to the Fratton area of Portsmouth to operate from Guildford Road where it was run by his grandmother. The Gauntlett connection goes back to 1836 with a dairy business sited in Copnor, but by the 1920s they had moved out to Purbrook to cater for the rapidly increasing number of houses that were being erected over the hill. A dairy shop and a restaurant were soon added to the Gauntlett organization. With the 1958 amalgamation, Gauntlett & Walker expanded to not only cover Portsmouth, but also Fareham, Emsworth, Clanfield, and Hayling Island. A dairy side to the business expanded even further, with cheese and other produce being supplied to shops and caterers in Hampshire and West Sussex. Mr. Walker died in 1980, his widow, Mrs Honor Walker, relinquished her interest in the dairy business in order to concentrate on developing Hampshire Electrics, a specialist company catering for the sales and service of electric vehicles. The dairy side has continued under the title of Gauntlett Dairies Limited, so this old name has not disappeared from the local scene completely.

Another dairy partnership, that of Hoar & Dumbrill, is one that features strongly in Portsmouth dairy history. In the early days of this century H & D had 47 handcarts delivering milk around Portsmouth, and they also used horse-drawn carts at times, for which the partners bought their ponies cheaply from the New Forest, it is understandable that the weight of the fully loaded milk carts soon succeeded in breaking the ponies in, then they would flog the horses off at a profit and go and get some more, shades of animal exploitation.

The name we associate with Hoar & Dumbrill is that of Bowditch, for Charles Bowditch worked as a milkman for them for 33 years, starting in 1907. Charlie's son Henry also joined the firm as a milkman, and he has fond memories of delivering milk around Portsmouth in the pre-war days, in fact it was through working for H & D that he met his wife Ena, who worked in the offices. Henry had to be an early-riser in those days, for in the early hours he had to drive a truck down to the Town Station to collect milk from the milk-train. It paid to be early, for the railway porters could help him load up, but if he was any later the fish train would steam in to command the porters' attention. As some of the churns weighed over 2 cwt., humping them about on your own was no mean task. The trucks that H & D used were old solid-tyred Thorneycroft's. relics from the First World War.

The Hoar & Dumbrill dairy depot was more like a factory, for they also produced their own butter and cream there. It is interesting to note that the milk that went off was sold cheaply to members of the Jewish fraternity for making cheese and unleavened bread. Many residents living near the depot would complain about the excessive noise, and one may imagine that the clanking of milk bottles in the early hours of the morning could do little for your beauty sleep, but there was not much that they could do about it for the dairy was there long before the houses were built.

The milkmen had to work up their own rounds, and if they left they very often took the round with them, so if a H & D milkman left to work for Street's Dairies, the latter gained a round, and H & D lost one. Not many milkmen could afford holidays in those days, but if they did manage to save enough money to take a break they had to arrange their own relief milkman. Not that this was a problem, for there were always plenty of unemployed chaps only too pleased to earn a week's wages. John Elias Dumbrill died in 1922 at the age of 76, but the Hoar & Dumbrill name carried on until the war, when bombs badly damaged the main depot in Somers Road. Henry Bowditch had left the milk trade just prior to the war, going to work for Cammell Laird. He has now retired and lives in Cosham, and I am indebted for him for his milk memories.

Our milk round is almost over, but here are a few more dairy names from the past that readers may remember. I mentioned Street's Dairies a few lines back; operating from Duncan Road, they were quite a go-ahead firm, in fact they were one of the first dairies to introduce glass milk bottles. This was an American trend that gradually came to this country, but many of the old-established dairies in the area were not keen on the bottles in their early days. Competing with Street's we had Stretton & Somerset Dairy, the Brooklands Dairy, Bladen Dairies of Eastney, Miles Dairy of Albert Road, the Dorset Pure Milk Supply Company, Short & Sons, James Bruce & Son, Tom Capper & Son, James Gardner & Son, Taylor & Son, Moore & Son, Young & Son, and the Allen Brothers. By the number of "Sons" in the above names, one can get some idea of what a family type business the dairy trade was then. The family name that dominated the Portsmouth milk scene for many years was that of Benham, with dairy shops at New Road, Inverness Road, Copythorn Road, and Copnor Road. The longest established of these was Bob Benham's branch in New Road.

In the 1920s milk was 3½d. a pint on the average, and for those who had a passion for cream, you could buy a carton of it for 3d. or 6d. If the thought of all that cream has not made you feel sick, then I am sure that those prices will! And that completes our tour around the Food Department of the Emporium, we must now turn our attention to what we refer to in the trade as "Dry Goods".

SHOP IN
PALMERSTON RD
OSBORNE RD. and CLARENDON RD.
SOUTHSEA.

Issued by the Traders to Broadcast the Merits of Palmerston, Clarendon and Osborne Roads, Southsea

Where Everybody Shops

Handley's Corner, c.*1906.*

Palmerston Road and Handley's in festive mood.

First Floor
Drapery–Fashions–Tailoring–Underwear–Footwear etc.

Welcome to the First Floor! Out of breath eh? You should have taken the lift like me! You are now in my world, "Dry Goods". I say that because for a good portion of my life I appear to have been engaged in selling goods such as furniture, hardware, menswear, drapery, fashions, and even ladies unmentionables! What are they? Sorry, I am not going to mention them!

Appearance was looked upon as a prime essential in days gone by, and to make sure their staff maintained a smart appearance, store managers would line them up for inspection every morning before the main doors were opened. This scrutiny could be of the "Nitty Nora" school variety, even finger nails were not ignored by the eagle-eyed floor walkers.

Serving behind a counter calls for the patience of a saint, the diplomacy of a politician, the rebound ability of Pearl White, and the stamina of Red Rum! Renowned writer H.G. Wells would have verified this, for he served an apprenticeship from 1881 to 1883 at Edwin Hide's drapery store on the corner of St. Paul's and King's Road. By the way, Mr. Hide also deserves mention for his good work in assisting the forwarding of the Portsmouth High School for Girls, and for giving local lads some chance of obtaining a commercial education. Anyway, it was not a particularly happy period for the young Wells, for without a public library he was dependent on the Y.M.C.A. at Landport for books and other forms of mental food. Eventually, he was able to hang up his tape measure and move to a teaching post at Midhurst Grammar School, but his drapery experience did provide him with background material for some of his best-selling books, notably "The Wheels of Chance" and the "History of Mr. Polly".

In the last century a drapery assistant's lot was not a happy one, with most shops being open until late evening. The drapers of Portsmouth in 1825 attempted to enforce some form of control of opening hours; at a large meeting it was unanimously decided that drapers would close their shops at 8 o'clock on winter evenings, and at 9 o'clock in the summer. This could hardly have gone any way towards cheering-up the hard worked assistants, who were left with little time for leisure.

Although in my time I have not been adverse to measuring out the odd yard of elastic, or to even serving Madam with a size 36B cup, I have decided to draw on the experiences of my old friend Jackie Facy to provide for readers some idea of what it was like to be a departmental store assistant in the 1920s and 30s, for she spent most of her working life in the rag and drapery trade.

An apprenticeship usually lasted two years, in which time the assistant generally had a few months' experience in each department. Most people dread having the book thrown at them, but young shop assistants did not mind, for it meant that they had made a promising start to their career. The "book" in question was awarded when it was thought that they were efficient enough, and they kept it for the duration of their employment. It had your number on the front, and inside it held a headed bill pad with fifty duplicated pages. When the fifty had been used, there was the ordeal of going to the cash desk and signing a form to get another pad. There were generally three assistants to a counter, although the Manchester Department, the name for sheets, towels etc., could have as many as six serving. The First Assistant always served customers first, the Second Assistant took over when called on to do so, and only when. These latter assistants were usually newly-trained apprentices. Of course, on busy Saturdays and Sale days the procedure was more loosely adhered to, for they were often called upon to serve several customers at once. The art of it was in trying to keep everybody happy, so assistants asked Madam what she wanted, got a tray out for her to look through, then served other customers.

It was a sin to lose a sale, if you could not make a sale, you referred Madam to your First Sales Assistant, and if she could not satisfy Madam she called the Buyer. This was rather like calling in the heavy gang, for the Buyer would use the hard-sell to induce the customer to buy something she did not really want in the first place. After the customer had slunk out of the store wondering what she was going to tell her "old man" when she got home, the Buyer would turn on the assistants and tell them off for not trying hard enough to make a sale. Buyers were usually tough old spinster ladies who had gained their experience in other big stores, they always wore black stockings, and they always had a tape measure and scissors on a belt around their waists. Rank certainly held sway in a large departmental store, it was rather like the Army with Privates, Corporals, Sergeants, and Officers, but for those substitute Assistants, First Assistants, Buyers, and Floor-Walkers. The Floor-Walker usually wore a black pin-striped suit, held open the doors for prospective customers, and bowed them out if they made a purchase.

Jackie Facy remembers that they were told to always make sure that the customer was given the bag with the printed side proclaiming the stores name on the outside, thus turning them into a walking advertisement. Without wishing to turn this book into a "Confessions of a Shop Assistant" style promotion, I would nevertheless like to reveal some of Jackie's recollections about the tricks of trade that were exploited in those days. Most purchases had three farthings on the end, but instead of the farthing change the customer would be given a packet of pins in lieu. This practice really provided the store with more profit, for the pins were not worth a farthing! But the assistants also became switched on, and they made a point of asking the customer if she wanted the pins, to which she usually replied: "No, you can keep the farthing". The farthing was put into a special box under the counter, and at the end of the month it was shared out amongst the assistants of that department. Jackie recalls that she sometimes got as much as a whole shilling!

One of the most devious tricks used in a store was implemented at SALE times; in the weeks leading up to the event certain assistants were delegated to a place that was out of the public's eyes, then they had the task of taking off tickets, putting the price up with a black pen, crossing it through with a red pen, then writing on the original price in red so that it looked like a genuine reduction! Readers will realize at this point why I am not actually naming any stores!

One customer can be easy enough to handle, but two together can produce problems. Jackie recalls one incident in which she was serving two ladies, one of them was getting impatient with the other one who was trying to make up her mind. The rather posh lady said: "Are you aware that I am an Account Customer"? to which the other lady replied: "Account Customer? That is just a posh name for Tick, I always pay with cash, so I deserve more attention!" But even this pales with the story regarding two other lady customers that Jackie was attempting to serve. They were arguing over which of them had the first claim on a dress that they both fancied, the conversation got very heated and could be heard all over the store. Eventually, the Buyer stepped forward, then to everyone's amazement she calmly produced scissors and cut the dress into two, saying: "There you are, ladies"!

On a wage of thirty-bob a week, sometimes less, a shop assistant could not exactly be expected to whoop-it-up in off-duty hours, but it was experience that money can't buy. This was fully realized by Jackie Facy and her husband Norman when they started their own drapery and outfitting business, apprenticeships are vital in producing standards that can only enhance the customer and

1905, Commercial Road and the Landport Drapery Bazaar.

BRIGHT'S
CORNER
PHONE 3572
LATE FLORA.
BRIGHT'S
BRIGHT'S
BRIGHT'S
CIRCULATING
LIBRARY
in connection with
The Times Book Club.
Free Country Delivery.
Write for Prospectus.
Rest and Reading Room
Second Floor. Electric Lift.
The Southsea
House of Fashion
Day and Evening Gowns,
Wraps, Costumes, Millinery,
Lingerie, Knitwear, Furs,
Gloves, Hosiery, Umbrellas,
Scarves, Bags & Fancy Goods
BRIGHTS
SOUTHSEA LTD
PALMERSTON RD & OSBORNE RD
SOUTHSEA.

salesperson relationship, something that is sadly lacking in the "Self-Service" world we now live in.

From Rags to Stitches

Although many businesses in Portsmouth started off purely as drapers, as they expanded they began to develop other lines such as tailoring, outfitting, furnishing and hardware, in fact anything that would reap a profit. In the forty years prior to the Second World War the city had an abundance of such establishments, businesses that began as one small shop and developed into massive departmental stores. It will only be a drop in the ocean, but I hope by mentioning a few of these names from the past I may impart some degree of pleasure to the reader.

When I announce the name of John Dyer, it is quite likely that it will produce a multitude of blank expressions, and yet, in those balmy pre-1939 days it was quite rightly proclaimed as "Southsea's Greatest Store" with over sixty departments catering for the customer's every whim. It all began in 1862, when an enterprising chap named John Dyer, who was Portsmouth born and bred, opened a small drapery shop at No. 65, Wish Street, this being the old name for King's Road. Employing a staff of two assistants, the Dyer empire gradually expanded to takeover shops on the other side of the road, and from thereon the whole business mushroomed, with other shops and buildings being swallowed rapidly in the cause of growth. The drapery side was so successful, John cast his commercial eyes towards other goods, thus developing a huge house furnishing department. He even entered the funeral trade, providing a special building that had a private entrance in Bush Street to ensure privacy for mourners. The expansion went on and on, at one time it looked as if the John Dyer empire would encompass the whole of King's Road, for those who like figures I can reveal that the Dyer Emporium covered a fantastic 100,000 sq.ft. of selling space, in addition to which there were several departments for furniture removals and storage, carpets and lino, and cabinet making. They also had the contract for supplying carpeting to the Dockyard.

During the heyday of the John Dyer concern, the 1920s, orchestras would play for shoppers in the morning from 12 to 1-30pm., then again in the afternoon from 3-45 for two hours. Many gimmicks were introduced to attract prospective customers, with mindreading and palmistry proving most popular. In 1923 Prof. J. Millott Severn drew large audiences at Dyer's with his demonstration of phrenology, and if you crossed the Professor's palm with half-a-crown, he would give you an instant character reading. Believe it or not, bookings were heavy for his services, and many folk were disappointed by the end of the week that they had not been able to experience his powers. A lady named Madame Toogood was also a regular attraction there, giving demonstrations and advice on corsets in relation to figure and health, but more about that subject later.

I have reason to believe that lurking in the darkest depths of most departmental stores there is a little man fully occupied with thinking up sales slogans, and apart from their claim to be the greatest store in Southsea, Dyer's favoured a slogan that announced from up high: "A Day Well Spent, Brings A Deal of Content." Well, John Dyer was quite content anyway, as long as the tills kept ringing. And fortunately for him they did, with customers coming from far and wide. They also operated a delivery service with a 30 mile radius which incuded the Isle of Wight. John remained active in the business, although as he got older his son Luthor was on hand to keep things ticking over. But, it was all to end in 1941, and like so many other fine Portsmouth buildings, the John Dyer Emporium was crushed by Hitler's dreaded war machine. Unfortunately, unlike many of the other large stores that were demolished by bombing, Dyer's never arose from the rubble to regain their former glory.

We do not have far to go for our next object of commercial affection, for it is only a few minutes walk from King's Road to Palmerston Road. This really was the in-place in days gone by, shopping in Palmerston Road was as much a ritual as a Sunday afternoon stroll along Ladies' Mile, and the crossroads where Palmerston meets with Osborne Road was Southsea's answer to Piccadilly Circus. And yet, only 130 years ago that same area was adorned with a picturesque farmhouse and charming cottages, and was referred to as "The Village". The first houses built there were named Beresford Terrace, a site later occupied by Morant's and the National Provincial Bank. By the 1860s Southsea residents were complaining about the bad state of the local roads, and Palmerston Road was known as Palmerston Swamp.

But let us return to those crossroads, and to one corner of it in particular. Yes, Handleys Corner. For over one hundred years this revered establishment was not just another store, it was an institution. When George Handley opened his drapery store in 1869 it faced open fields, and even George could not have possibly envisaged the growth of the area, and his shop in particular. But grow it did, beginning with only one assistant, George was gradually able to expand into adjacent premises and increase his staff numbers. As Southsea expanded into a popular watering place, so Handley's expanded with it. George was helped to a great extent by gathering about him a loyal and dedicated band of workers, one of them being a young chap named George Hayward, who joined the Handley store in the 1870s. He became one of the Guvnor's right-hand men, and completed over fifty years service in the store. Needless to say, when George Hayward died in 1928, Handley's carried out the funeral arrangements. Loyal to the end!

George Handley himself had died a couple of years before this, he passed away at his home at Seaview on the Isle of Wight in 1926 in his 80th year. Fortunately, by this time his three sons, Douglas, George, and Trevor had gained a good grounding in the business, and under their guidance Handley's growth continued apace. Like John Dyer's down the road, no gimmick was left untried in the fight to attract customers through the front doors. The attractions included a roof garden, lending library, a magnificient restaurant, even a zoo! And of course, there was always the sound of music above the tinkling of the cash registers, provided by several well known London orchestras. But there is no doubt as to who took the vote for the most colourful musical group to appear at Handley's, this just had to be the Gypsy Band, dressed in full gypsy outfits they would stroll amongst the shoppers playing tear-jerking little numbers on their violins. Well, it meant good business for the handkerchief counter anyway!

The competition between the big Southsea stores was particularly fierce during the Christmas period, each vying to put on the greatest attraction. For the 1925 season John Dyer's really went to town, the store was transformed into a huge wonderland complete with a fairy cottage, very pretty indeed. Not to be outdone, the Landport Drapery Bazaar had a full-blown Japanese Village for their party-piece, with masses of coloured lanterns to set the scene. But neither store had reckoned on Handley's, for with an eye to the future their Christmas attraction was simply years ahead, it had a rocket style theme that was featured as a "Space Trip to Mars". The word soon got about, and hordes of Portsmouth children pestered their Mums and Dads until they took them to Handley's. "Urghh, I want to get out. Mum, I feel sick!"

Handley's sold just about everything, and I really do mean everything. "Good morning Sir, have you seen our latest range in aircraft?" Yes, it's true, taking advantage of the opening of Portsmouth Airport in 1932, and the new-found enthusiasm for flying, Handley's actually sold aeroplanes, and even had one on show in the Southsea store. A Redwing two-seater aircraft could be bought for £650. Hire Purchase terms available on request. "Oh, and by the way Sir, while you are up there flying over Portsmouth, would you mind scattering this bag of 25,000 leaflets advertising our next sale!"

If they sold planes, it was only natural that they also sold cars, and they did in fact have a flourishing motor department. Whilst on the subject of transport, I think this would be a good moment to call upon the memories of Cyril Stares, for he was very much involved with transport matters at Handley's in the old days. Cyril started work there in 1918 at the age of 13, commencing as a van boy in the delivery department. At that time horse-drawn vehicles were still being used, plus a number of 3-wheeled bicycle vans. Motor vans were gradually introduced to allow coverage of a wide radius around Portsmouth, including the Isle of Wight. Cyril recalls that they ran a daily service to the Island, the vans going over on the old cattle boats. It was a tricky business getting the vehicles on to the boat in those days, without the modern aid of drive-on, drive-off, they had to reverse the vans over two planks in order to board the vessel.

As motoring got more popular, Cyril Stares progressed to working in Handley's garage. In the 20s they had a large garage in Portland Street where cars could be left there all day for a charge of one shilling and whilst you were going about your shopping, your car could be cleaned and polished, 2/6d. for washing, and 1/6d. for polishing. Petrol and oil were also available, and small repairs while you waited, or preferably shopped.

Handley's staff were well looked after, with many of the young girls actually living on the premises whilst they served their apprenticeships. There was a staff social club available at nearby Dovercourt in Kent Road. Known as the Highbank Club, it provided tennis courts, billiards, and even a concert party. Staff were even provided with the services of the resident store chiropodist, Mr. Edgar Green, who had a knack for reviving tired and aching tootsies. In their leisure hours, staff were able to read the Handley house magazine, it was produced monthly and was cunningly called "Handleaves". It contained a variety of information and helpful hints, such as tips about how to detect any dud coins passed over the counter, or dropping gentle reminders that staff who made a practice of arriving late for work were being closely watched! Shades of Big Brother!

The customers were also provided with something to read, this came in the form of a weekly amusement guide that proclaimed the wonderous attractions of Portsmouth and Southsea, and even provided local bus and tram time-tables. The issue for the week commencing 6 April 1925 informs us that Gertie Gitana is appearing at the Hippodrome in a new revue called "Nellie Dean". Film fans could visit the Majestic in Kingston Road to gasp at the exploits of Rudolph Valentino in "Monsieur Beaucaire", or laugh themselves silly at the antics of Buster Keaton in "Sherlock Junior" at the Arcade Cinema. By the way, the amusement guide lists the programmes of no fewer than ten Portsmouth cinemas that particular week, plus five stage productions at the local theatres.

Cyril Stares has fond memories of the annual outings at Handley's, sometimes they involved nearly 500 members of staff being transported around the countryside by a fleet of charabancs. Not wishing to lose valuable Saturday morning business, the outings never got under way until the afternoon. Each departmental head was put in charge of a charabanc. "Stop giggling at the back there!" The youngsters could hardly help but giggle, because for every day of their working year they were accustomed to seeing their departmental heads wearing rather dark and solemn clothes, and the sight of them togged out in cloth caps, grey flannels, and white plimsolls, made giggling very hard to suppress! Regular staff outings at Handley's began in 1922, but I have chosen the June 1926 outing to give readers some idea of what they got up to. At 1-30 sixteen Southdown coaches arrived to be boarded by 450 members of staff, fortunately, at that moment the sun came out. The first stop was Slindon Woods, then they proceeded to Midhurst for tea, following which they visited Cowdray Park for sports. This included tug-o-war with Ladies v. Gents, and a mixed cricket match, then there was dancing in the park, with the Charleston proving most popular. Sadly, it was soon time to start the journey home, with of course a few pub stops along the way, then it was back to work on Monday, meaning you had to wait another year before you could see that dashing young chap from the China Department in his cloth cap and braces again!

Cyril Stares left Handley's to work for Park's the Portsmouth carriers, but he has never forgotten his happy working days of youth in the great Southsea store. A few more prosperous shopping years were to pass, then came the war, and that dreaded night 10 January 1941. Handley's was badly hit, and the staff and firefighters could only stand and stare in horror as this magnificent building crumbled down, for enemy action had cut off the water supply. The light of day revealed the mangled wreckage that had once been Handley's. But, a few weeks after the dust had died down, they were back in business, operating from small shops in the area that had managed to escape demolition. After the war building materials were in short supply, with priority being given to the building of homes, and it was not until the 1950s that re-building commenced. The great day arrived in 1955, with the Lord Mayor of Portsmouth, Mr. G.A. Day, officially declaring the new Handley's Store well and truly opened. In the following years the store continued to flourish, maintaining good standards as always, but being adaptable enough to keep up with modern trends and so survive into the 1980s. The only thing that has really changed is the name. It is part of the vast Debenham empire. But, whatever name is affixed to the fascia, for most older inhabitants of Portsmouth and Southsea that part of Palmerston Road will always lovingly be known as Handley's Corner.

The Dynamic Duo

When we think of Laurel & Hardy, we think of Hollywood. When we think of Tate & Lyle, we think of sugar. When we think of Knight & Lee, it is fairly certain we will think of Southsea, for this dynamic drapery duo formed a partnership that still remains a household word on the South Coast, sixty years after they personally went to work for that "Great Draper in the Sky". Strangely enough, the founding of the business cannot be attributed to either Mr. Knight or Mr. Lee, the credit for this must go to Mr. Wink, known to his friends as William. William set up as a "Lacemaker" in 1831, working from premises in Queen Street. When he died in 1857, the business was carried on by Sarah Wink, presumably his widow. White's Directory lists Sarah as operating from 112, Queen Street, and she came under the category of "lace manufacturer, milliner, and dressmaker". By 1865 the business was under the name of Frederick Wink, the shop front proclaiming "Wink & Co. Silk Mercers & Ladies Outfitters". With an eye to expanding his trade, Frederick Wink moved to Palmerston Road in 1874, taking over premises that had been run by the Couzens family as two businesses, one being a seedsman and florist, the other a beerhouse. Seeds and booze were replaced by mantles, costumes, and drapery.

And so we reach the year of 1887, now this is where the story really begins, enter Mr. Knight and Mr. Lee. Jesse Knight and Edward Lee were friends who had worked together in the London store of William Whiteley. Wishing to start up on their own, they bought out the Southsea business of Wink & Co. The two friends, who later became brothers-in-law when Jesse married Edward's sister, widened the range of merchandise, one of their first innovation's being to open a department for boys' clothing, quickly followed by one for men's wear and military tailoring. Using retailing methods that could be deemed as revolutionary for those times, the business expanded shop by shop to put Knight & Lee well and truly on the Southsea shopping map.

The business became a private company in 1899, with the two founders continuing as directors with annual salaries of £1,000 each. The store itself was managed by Mr. H.E. Brown, a very capable gentlemen who like the two partners had previously worked in London with Whiteley's. Then came the 1914–18 war, which apart from the odd zeppelin flying over passed fairly peacefully for Knight & Lee's. It is interesting to recall that in 1915 the store was doing a good trade in officers Service uniforms, and were pushing the fact that they only used the best khaki cloth available. On the other hand, or perhaps I should say on the other side of the road, Handley's appeared to favour the Navy, blue serge proving to be their favourite colour of the year. Handley's also sold officer's swords, and you could purchase a good quality ornamental sword for only 45/-. If you fancied doing your Swinging Sumurai bit, all you had to do was to take your Handley sword across to Knight & Lee's and buy a special line in kimonos that had just arrived direct from Japan, yours for only 3/11d. I hope readers have noted that I have refrained from stating that the swords at 45/- were a cut-price offer!

Jessie Knight died at his Fareham home in 1922, and his partner and friend Edward Lee followed him a couple of years later. By this time profits were dropping, and the store was in pretty bad shape. Early 1925 saw the resignation of the Managing Director, Mr. H.E. Brown, and the Company Secretary. Mrs Knight and Mrs Lee attempted to keep the store open, praying for a buyer. Two well-known Portsmouth drapers to whom the business was offered declined to buy, but fortunately there was a saviour on hand to save the day, this was in the form of a Mr. Wilkinson who had previously been with Harrods. Under his guidance, Knight & Lee's began trading positively once again, for a few years anyway. But it was back to the doldrums in 1930, Wilkinson resigned, taking his financial support with him, causing the firm to borrow money to repay him. The store borrowed more money in 1931 in order to modernize. By 1933 they had a huge overdraft and were in desperate need of help. Don't worry folks, each cloud has a silver lining, and this one came in the form of the John Lewis Partnership, which having spread to the provinces to takeover such stores as Tyrrell & Green in Southampton, and Jessop's in Nottingham, took Knight & Lee under its wing in 1934.

After five years of successful trading, disaster struck in the early war years. Yes, that dreaded night of January the 10th, akin to their competitors the Knight & Lee emporium was completely destroyed. After getting over the initial shock, offices were set up in the Queen's Hotel, allowing all staff to be paid two weeks' money. This had to be calculated from memory as all the records had been destroyed in the bombing raid. The workers then went home to await further orders. These came at the end of February in 1941, when business was resumed in premises in the Palmerston Arcade. After the war they managed to acquire other properties in which to house their various departments, but they had to wait a little longer than Handley's to regain the large departmental store status that they had gained prior to the war. March 1959 saw the completion of the new Knight & Lee store on the corner opposite Handley's, the old site where they were bombed was filled by stores such as Woolworth's and Boots. With all their departments under one roof, except for the menswear shop, Knight & Lee's were back once again in the league of top stores in Portsmouth and Southsea. Although still under the control of the John Lewis Partnership, I am pleased that the Knight & Lee name has been retained, and I hope that they will continue to flourish from this corner of Southsea. One thing is certain, if it loses stores of the calibre of Knight & Lee's and Debenham's, Southsea will die as a shopping centre.

When Knight & Lee's and Handley's were demolished in 1941, another renowned store nearby also perished in the same raid,

Knight & Lee, Palmerston Road, c.1912.

that popular drapery and fashion house known as Morants in Palmerston Road. This store stood on the site upon which the new Knight & Lee store was erected in the 1950s. J.D. Morant's establishment before the war engendered a rather elite image, as their advertising would verify with statements such as "Don't look like the other woman", or "Where the discriminating may be clad".

That particular corner of the crossroads will become known as Knight & Lee's Corner, as will the old Handley's Corner on the other side be referred to as Debenham's Corner, but on the other corner in Osborne Road there was yet another famous landmark, this was known as Bright's Corner. This title was derived from the large departmental store that graced the corner in the pre-war years, Bright's of Southsea. It was a magnificent building, in appearance rather like the old Knight & Lee store on the corner of Stanley Lane. Akin to Morant's, Bright's purported to be a mecca of ladies fashions, but they also specialized in drapery, millinery, and fancy goods. Like Handley's they had a large circulating library, and a rest and reading room, plus the very latest electric lift.

Whilst talking about drapers, older readers may recall another well-known corner of the town, Marshall's Corner in Norfolk Street. This was another establishment that started as a small corner shop in 1907, the proud owner being Mr. Charles Marshall. The premises had previously served as a pianoforte shop, but all that Charles could play was the cash register, and this he did exceedingly well, for in next to no time he had two shops staffed by six lady assistants. But it did not stop there, by 1914 Marshall & Co. had eight shops employing 80 ladies. Also in 1914 he established his own shopping arcade with no less than twelve display windows on the corner of Hyde Street. As some of us may now wonder what happened to the Glorious British Empire, so we might ponder how such a concern as large as Marshall's could disappear, but I am afraid that by the outbreak of war it had indeed vanished from the Southsea shopping scene.

I am pleased to say that the next drapery departmental store was one of those that arose once again from the brick rubble of the war years, I should think there is hardly a reader who has not heard of the Landport Drapery Bazaar, for the name of this store has only changed in recent years. The L.D.B. story began back in 1865 when an enterprising gentleman named Robert Davies opened a drapery store on the corner of Arundel Street and Commercial Road, catering mostly for the many naval families that resided in Portsmouth then. Mr. Davies was only to survive for five years, for in 1870 the store was taken over by Mr. John Parkhouse, a go-ahead young chap who like Mr. Knight and Mr. Lee had gained his drapery experience in the West End of London. John was full of "bright" ideas, in fact he was one of the first shopkeepers in Portsmouth to have the new electric light installed in his premises. But another one of his brain-waves did not go down too well, this was when he showed the courage to actually display ladies corsets in his front windows, an act that drew loud cries of protest from many respectable citizens of the town. Oh well, you can't win them all. I wonder what those folk of one hundred years ago would think about the sexy lingerie that is paraded in full public view in most chain stores today?

Anyway, corsets or no corsets, the Parkhouse empire developed into a huge commercial success, and John Parkhouse was able to find places for his three sons in the business, Ernest, Horace, and William Parkhouse. Under their influence, the Landport Drapery Bazaar underwent many changes in the 1920s, alterations that turned it into one of the finest stores in the South. Like Handley's, a resplendent restaurant was added, complete with obligatory orchestra. The new image went down well with the customers, who came to visit L.D.B. from far and wide. It was a happy place to work, and akin to the other large stores the staff enjoyed a good off-duty social life, one of the many highlights being the annual staff outing. I mentioned previously that Handley's in 1926 went to Midhurst for their outing, and I was rather surprised to learn that the Parkhouse family led 300 of their staff on an outing to Midhurst also in the same year. One can only surmise how embarrassing it would have been if the two parties had met face to face in the main street at Midhurst, with perhaps the prospect of a pillow fight to make the day! Anyhow, during their splendid tea at Midhurst Mr. Parkhouse took the opportunity to award a special certificate of merit to Miss Barnes for her services in the underclothing department. No doubt it was for her undercover work!

But the merrymaking, and the moneymaking, were severely curtailed in January 1941, for yet again bombs had stopped play. The Landport Drapery Bazaar was flattened to rubble like most of its Commercial Road neighbours that night, and they had to continue trading from several small premises as a temporary measure to keep in business. But, as history has shown, they came back in a blaze of glory, with a new superstore being opened on the original site in 1955. The Parkhouse dreamstore was to suffer another setback in the early 60s, when a big fire caused a great deal of damage. But it was not long before large notices proclaiming "Fire Sale" were put on display, and L.D.B. was soon back in it's stride. In 1982 the store was given a huge face-lift inside and out, plus a new name. The L.D.B. banner was replaced by that of Allders, a subsidary company of the United Drapery Stores Group who had taken over L.D.B. originally in 1965. But whatever its name, Allders, Landports, or L.D.B., the fine tradition begun by John Parkhouse will I am sure be maintained for many years to come.

In the Commercial Road of the inter-war years there were quite a number of stores trading in drapery, ladies fashions, and fancy goods. In that number we might include names such as McIlroy's, the Premier Providing Company, and Weston Burt. Apart from John Dyer's, King's Road could also boast a good number of such emporia, including Arthur Bull, Drinkwater's, and Bulpitt's. The latter are of course still fondly remembered for the famous Bulpitt Newsletters that appeared in the *Portsmouth Evening News* for many years, they were so chatty and friendly it was hard to realize that they were really only adverts. John Bulpitt inherited the business from his father, Joseph, who had founded the family drapery concern in the 1880s. John became a Director of Bulpitt's Limited when the firm was incorporated in 1911, and two years later in 1913 he became Managing Director. An ardent member of the Rotary Club, he was also well known for his work in connection with the development of Boy Scout Association in Portsmouth. Bulpitt's were never left behind when it came to banging the drum, for whenever the N.U.T., National Union of Teachers, came to Portsmouth for their annual conferences, they were quick off their mark with their advertising, with banners announcing "At Bulpitt's we provide extra quality and value, because we know that teachers 'Never Use Trash' ". The N.U.T. being in bold lettering. This was in the pre-war days; after the war they continued trading at Osborne Road, moving to a spiffing new store in Palmerston Road in 1951. They also had branches at North End and Lee-on-the-Solent. John Bulpitt died in 1962 at the age of 80.

Mention of North End a few lines back reminds me of dear old Will Brown's establishment there, operating from Twyford Avenue and later London Road. Will also had a great deal of faith in the power of advertising, declaring that his drapery and outfitting could not be beaten for "Value, Service, & Variety". Given the choice and space for three more drapery names, I would list Frank Gosden of New Road, John Barnes of Fratton Road, and the London Drapery Stores in Albert and Lake roads. But of course, there were many, many, more.

Heads and Tales

There is no doubt about it, the shopkeepers of yesteryear showed far more finesse than their counterparts of today. So very often today we see large bold signs stating: "SALE – CLOSING DOWN – EVERYTHING MUST GO!" In earlier times they displayed a much more genteel approach, with a nicely written showcard in the window informing us: "We regret to inform customers that our premises are to close very shortly, the Proprietors would like to take this opportunity to sincerely thank regular patrons for their esteemed custom. We beg to point out that in order to clear our stocks we still have a selection of high quality goods to dispose of at considerably reduced prices!" You see what I mean.

But, as far as fashions go, a similar comparison may be made between the modern and the old-fashioned girl. Ladies clothes appear so brash and blatant now, with skirts being replaced by tight jeans that look as if they have been soaked in the bath for three months, and blouses replaced by equally tight T–shirts that have motifs such as "Non-Smokers Do It Without Puffing" emblazoned across the front. One of the few occasions we have nowadays to see ladies displaying some degree of elegance is in TV programmes such as "Come Dancing", you know the sort of thing: "Gladys is a part-time plumbers-mate from Bethnal Green, she has made her own costume, which contains 3,000 sequins and 2,000 metal bottle-tops!"

Ah! yes, they had more "savoir-faire" in the old days. I have in my possession a delightful magazine called the *Lady's Pictorial*, dated 1894. Although it was a national publication, it contains splendid mention of the festivities that took place in Southsea that particular season, and goes to great lengths to describe what the ladies who attended were wearing. For instance – "Dr. & Mrs J.R. Robertson were 'At Home' at their residence, Mayfield, Western Parade, Southsea, to some 200 guests. The charming hostess, Mrs Robertson, received her numerous guests in the drawing-room which was profusely decorated with flowers. She was wearing a gown in reseda green cloth, embroidered with a tiny pink spot, the bodice was made with a gathered vest of pink silk edged at the sides with folded pleats of myrtle green bengaline, the latter material draping at the waist as a sash, and fichu frills of the cloth lined with pink silk gave a very pretty finish to the bodice, whilst the skirt was trimmed with bands of green bengaline laid in zig-zag fashion". Wow! I should think they needed a fork-lift truck to get her into the room! But, just imagine about one hundred other ladies at this gathering dressed in similar fashion, it must have made a most colourful and splendid sight. You did not have any problems distinguishing men from women in those days!

Whatever happened to ladies' hats? In days gone by they would not have dared to go out in the street without one, and I suppose the same could be said about men, although personally I rarely venture out without my old straw boater. Today, hats appear to be objects of mirth, they are on display in ladies shops, but females seem to get great delight in facing a mirror and trying on the hats until they and everyone about them are helpless with laughter. In the old days hats were a very serious business, and you dare not show the semblance of a smile in case the proprietress of the establishment should see you and take offence. These ladies were always dressed in the height of fashion, and were generally afforded the title of Madame.

So, where did ladies buy their headgear in days gone by? I have already mentioned Will Brown's, Bulpitt's, and various departmental stores, and millinery emporiums included Madame Fritz in Palmerston Road, Madame Haine in Clarendon Road, Madame June in Clarendon Road, Madame Cossentine of Fawcett Road, Dorothy Permayne of Milton, Munro & Chetwood of King's Road, and Burns & Tier of New Road. To complete this list there is one name that most lady readers will be familiar with, that of

Dorothy Cooper. Dorothy was indeed the Queen of Hats, with branches in Elm Grove, Albert Road, London Road, Lake Road, Highland Road, Fratton Road, as well as Cosham and Gosport. What else can I say but "Hats off to Dorothy". Oh! and by the way, if you required a handbag to go with your new hat a good spot to visit was Elm Grove, for once there you had the choice of Thomas Webb's, or James Watkins.

Living off the Fat of the Land or **"Stay" As Sweet as you Are.** In my nostalgic ramblings about local history and industry, I have reached a very definite conclusion concerning Portsmouth. If Nottingham is renowned for its lace, Luton for its hats, Northampton for its footwear, then Portsmouth must be famous for its corsets! Not that I am for one moment suggesting that the lovely ladies of old Pompey had to rely on the meat-packing industry in order to maintain their figures, it just happens that Portsmouth appeared to have a healthy number of corset and stay manufacturers through the years, in fact in the 1920s and 30s there were no fewer than 23 such factories living off the fat of the land.

As one strolled through the streets of Portsmouth and Southsea in the Victorian and Edwardian days, it was quite common to hear screams of agony amidst much grunting and groaning bursting forth from open windows. Don't worry, it was not Jack the Ripper down here on his hols, it was only the sounds of maids yanking heartily on laces in order to pack the squelching flesh of their mistresses into a particularly ferocious pair of corsets. The mistresses usually hanging on to the bedpost with great tenacity. All this suffering was in the cause of beauty, and I can only hope that the pain was worth it at the end of the day, or night! Another way in which one might find it easier to fit into a corset was by visiting the local massage parlour and having surplus flesh pounded away. Don't laugh, I am quite serious, readers might be surprised to learn that at one time Portsmouth could boast at least twelve massage parlours operating at the same time. For the genuine Swedish Massage the place to go was Gustaf Allbrandt's in St. David's Road, but before the "boys in blue" start plotting a police raid, I must explain that Gustaf is no longer with us. Madame Mona, who operated her massage parlour from Woodville in Florence Road, promised to make ladies more beautiful in the twinkling of a mud-pack, and specialized in the wonders of electrolysis.

But, enough of all this naughty talk about massage, let us get back to corsets. Male readers need not bypass any pages, for they were not adverse to wearing such garments in times gone by. William Furlong died in 1960 at the age of 95, and there was little doubt that William knew his corsets, for he had worked in the trade for over sixty years. He not only made them, but was also responsible for designing them as well. One particular item for which he was in popular demand was for stays made in silk and satin, these being for Guards and Cavalry Officers. No wonder they always looked so upright! Although as an old soldier, I was rather shocked to learn recently that many soldiers in the Army of today wear ladies tights under their trousers whilst carrying out sentry duty on cold nights! I always said "There was something about a Soldier".

Oh! well, let us get down to naming a few names. How about "Twilfit" for a start? This household name was founded by a gentleman named Colonel C.L. Reynolds, who after gaining experience in the corset trade at an early age began his own business at the ripe old age of 18 by opening a factory in Canal Walk in 1844. Beginning with a staff force of 50, the business continued to expand into this century, and in the 1920s that staff figure had multiplied considerably with 1,200 hands turning out two and a quarter million corsets a year. In the last century premises were opened in Sultan Road, then they expanded to additional factories in Grosvenor Street and Kingston by 1889.

Elm Grove Post Office in the 1920s.

Skeens & Paine, Elm Grove.

Osborne Road.

Porter Brothers annual outing, 1913.

John Dyer's Emporium, King's Road, 1905.

There was strong competition from German manufacturers in those days; to combat this another factory was acquired in Landport Street, accompanied by a massive advertising campaign and a change of name to "Twilfit". The firm operated officially as Charles Leetham & Co. in the 1920s, with five factories in Arundel Street, King Street, Sultan Road, Mill Lane, and Highland road. The latter was known as the Marina Factory, and in the 20s they pioneered an attractive line in ladies brassieres, a vital piece of apparatus for females who had a passion for suddenly leaping into the Charleston.

"For the perfect outline, a Veco Corset is essential if you are to look your best". And of course the place to get your Veco corset was at Voller's, don't forget to ask for Model 131, a snip at 9/11d. This old established business was founded by the Voller family in 1897 at Kingston Road, and has passed on through the family. Over the years Voller's have produced an endless range of corsets, and I am pleased to say that they are still going strong in the 1980s, despite a bad fire in 1981 which destroyed stock and many historical records. I should also add that "Twilfit" flourished in Portsmouth at their factory in St. Mary's Road, as did the old established corset firm, the Hampshire Corset Company in Binsteed Road.

If you went into Alder's store in Lake Road in 1912, the model to ask for was No. 582, a special belted corset that was guaranteed to give satisfaction. Alder's, who also had a branch in Albert Road, did not pull any punches with their advertising, they boldly announced in large lettering that their garments "Improved Stout Figures". If the No. 582 was too expensive for you at 5/11d., you could pop down to Walter Gleave's shop in Arundel Street and buy one of his bargain corsets, yours for 2/11d. Walter also had branches in Commercial Road and The Arcade.

With a final flurry, I will submit for your approval a few more names of Portsmouth corset manufacturers. In the last century the firms to make their mark included J. Chilcot & Co. in Upper Surrey Street, Thomas Gould in Commercial Road, William Carter in Great Charlotte Street, William Helbt in Queen Street, and George Ward in Meadow Street. Moving into the earlier part of this century there were the Victoria Corset Company in Cardigan Road, Henry Plummer in Arundel Street, the Weingarten Brothers in All Saints Road, Edwin Izod in Commercial Place, William Fletcher in Hay Street, Charles Bayer in St. Mary's Road, and Madame Lee in Margate Road. Right, that is it, you can now take your corsets off. Go on, have a good scratch, I won't tell anybody!

Made to Measure

A young man ran into a tailor's shop and cried: "You must help me, I am desperate. I'm getting married tomorrow and I need a suit. Can you make me one"? The little man behind the counter gesticulated and exclaimed: "My life already, a suit by tomorrow! But for cash money, I will see what I can do".

And so, the next day the happy couple were walking down the aisle. On seeing her new son-in-law for the first time, the bride's mother gasped: "Oh no, nobody told me that he was a hunchback!" A relative next to her whispered in her ear: "He's no hunchback. That is the tailor still inside trying to finish the suit!"

I expect many chaps will have memories of the suit that they got married in, and I for one prefer not to think about mine, for in my wedding photographs I look more like a penguin doing a commercial for a well-known chocolate bar! It was a terrible fit, considering it was supposed to have been made to measure. And after all, it wasn't cheap, I paid four quid for that suit!

When people start thinking back to men's clothes in the past, it is fairly certain that before long the "Fifty-bob Tailor" will crop up, and although it now seems a very small sum to pay for a suit, it was still a lot of money in the 20s and 30s, in fact it was the average weekly wage. If you were lucky enough to have been in work! Many folk then begrudged forking out fifty-bob for a suit, for not so many years before you could get one for half this price. In 1912, Woolf Brothers at their tailoring shop in Commercial Road were advertising off-the-peg mens suits for only 20/-, or you could have one made to measure for 35/-. You could hardly get a tie for that now!

Unlike the world we now live in, where everyone tries to do everybody else's job, whether they have had any training or not, in the old days there were strong objections to moonlighting from your chosen profession. In the 1660s several cases were brought to court in Portsmouth, many concerning the tailoring trade. Aspiring tailors were severely dealt with by the magistrates for carrying out a trade for which they had not been apprenticed.

In order to find the first Portsmouth tailor that we shall be recalling we will have to go to the High Street of the 18th Century and look for the name of Melchizedek Meredith. This gentleman was the grandfather of George Meredith the famous novelist, George being born at No. 73 High Street in 1828. Although it would seem that the great writer escaped from Portsmouth at his first given opportunity, he did however draw on the town of his birth for his books, and modelled characters in the stories on his family. And what characters his family were, more colourful than fiction in many ways.

Melchizedek Meredith opened his High Street shop in 1785, and some of his first customers to have their inside leg measured included such notable seafaring names as Admiral Nelson, Collingwood, Rodney, Howe, and Jervis. How is that for a list of references? Melchizedek believed in living life to the full, with his tailoring business only serving to finance his great passion for wine, women, song, and horses. Anyway, the "Great Mel's" lifestyle eventually caught up with him, and he went to meet his Maker at the age of 51, leaving his son Augustus, George's father,

The new Gieves, Matthews & Seagrove Ltd. store, opened in 1909.

Handley's Garage, 1920s.

Ransom for hardware, Fawcett Road.

Ben Grubb, Commercial Road.

Handley's, January 1941.

to try and pick up the pieces of what was left of the family tailoring business.

In his youth, Augustus had aspirations of becoming a doctor, and had very little love for the tailoring trade. Although possessed of a more sober character than his father, he was by no means perfect, and it was due to his wife's ability that the shop was kept going. When she died, Augustus went to pieces, and the business was on the verge of bankruptcy. He took another wife and moved to London to try and make a fresh start, selling the business to a neighbouring tradesman, Joseph Galt. Trade began to look up, and in the 1850's Joseph was joined in partnership by James Gieve, a surname that many readers will be familiar with.

Galt & Gieve made it a partnership to remember, going from strength to strength over the following fifty years. Following amalgamations with other tailoring concerns in the early 1900s, the company became known as Gieves Limited, resulting in branches being opened in coastal towns such as Chatham, Weymouth, Devonport, Harwich and Sheerness. They specialized in naval and military tailoring, and had a branch in London. The rest is history, with the current concern of Gieves & Hawkes known and respected throughout the world for its association with the Royal Navy, a tradition that began with Nelson.

When Sir John Baker died in 1909, it was indeed a sad loss for Portsmouth, for he served for fifty years on the Coporation, was Mayor twice, and was notable for his good work in education, hospitals, and recreation. Indeed he was instrumental in the provision of Victoria Park. Amidst all these functions he somehow managed to find time to build a successful tailoring business, with branches in Commercial Road and Albert Road. I think the fact that he was known throughout Portsmouth as "Honest John" serves to indicate the inhabitants' feelings for him as a trader, and in public life. The first John Baker shop opened in 1860, twenty branches followed.

John Baker had plenty of competition in the 20s and 30s, for Commercial Road was Portsmouth's version of London's Saville Row, with an abundance of tailoring shops fighting it out with pattern book and tape measure. Just a few doors away from Baker's was the establishment of Beaumont's, a men's and boy's outfitting business that is still going strong in the 1980s. It all began when Charles Jersey Beaumont came to Portsmouth in 1878 from Jersey to open a naval tailors; the business is still run by the Beaumont family with over one hundred years of service to the public, expanding to branches all over the Portsmouth area.

Not many yards from Beaumont's the mammoth tailoring concern of Montague Burton was well in evidence, and just before the outbreak of war they had opened another branch nearby, in fact next to John Baker's. Just past Crasswell Street, but still in Commercial Road, there was a small tailor who sported a name that is more typical of the sort we associate with tailors, Woolf Swick. And a few doors away from Mr. Swick there was the well-known establishment of Porter Brothers, who modestly billed themselves as Southsea and Portsmouth's principal outfitters. In the 20s they certainly had popular prices at Porter's, with blazers in blue or brown from 16/6d., lounge suits from 63/-, flannel trousers from 14/11d., and shirts from 5/11d. I expect I would look a laughing stock now, but I always fancied myself in plus-fours for some odd reason, perhaps it is the sporting instinct in me. At 45/- for a plus-four suit, Porter's contended that they were asking a sporting price. They also had branches at Palmerston Road and Elm Grove, but by the mid-30s the Commercial Road shop had been taken over by J. Davidson, another popular tailor and outfitter.

I just love those old names, and to be honest if I could go back to when I started my literary ramblings, I would discard the mundane name of Ron Brown for something more outstanding. Given the chance, I would use a name such as Erastus Cracknell to add a touch of glamour. Now, the real Erastus Cracknell was not known for his literary work, but he was renowned for his old-established tailoring business in Elm Grove, a business that was founded in the early 1800s and flourished for well over one hundred years. Another old tailoring establishment is that of Moseley & Pounsford on Portsmouth Hard, and I am pleased to say that they are still flourishing as I put finger to typewriter.

Another clothing establishment that is still going strong is that of Robert Mack Ltd. in Charlotte Street, just the place for a pair of long johns or a sturdy pair of boots. It all began in 1929 when Joseph Mack opened a second-hand clothing store, which was taken over in 1932 by his son and daughter-in-law, Robert and Ethel Mack. They took over the premises next door in 1934 and expanded into ex-Government surplus supplies, a move that proved most successful. In addition to building their business, both Robert and Ethel managed to find time to serve on the Portsmouth City Council for many years. Robert died in 1961, and Ethel survived until 1977, their son Jack Mack carried on as Managing Director, and their grandson Michael Zeffertt joined the firm with his wife Sylvia. Mack's expanded by opening a branch at Southampton in 1978, and the Government surplus side of the business is augmented by industrial and leisure wear, and camping equipment.

Other memorable tailors included Goode the Tailors in Wickham Street, the West of England Clothing Association sited opposite the Town Station, Caffin & Son in King's Road, John Bright in Commercial Road, Lawson Foote in Victoria Road South, George Brown in Osborne Road, Read & Co also in Osborne Road, George Henry Purse in Campbell Road, and Thomas Triggs in New Road. And finally, a special mention for the family tailoring business of Ward's in Palmerston Road, the connection ending when Bernard Ward died in 1925. Bernard, who was a well-known local swimmer and had strong links with the Southsea Swimming Club, took the business over from his father, who was a much respected Portsmouth Alderman.

Now let me see, we have now kitted ourselves out in hats,

dresses, suits, shirts, and even corsets, but there still seems to be something missing? Ah! yes, you cannot go out into the street in bare feet, can you? So, follow me into the last department on the First Floor of the Emporium.

All God's Children got Shoes

In the winter when the ground was icy, do you remember how we used to make slides in the school playground, Cor, wasn't it fun? Mind you, it did not do the seat of my trousers or the soles of my shoes much good, and generally I finished up with getting a clip around the ear from Mum when I got home! Come to think of it, I always seemed to have the bottom hanging out of my trousers or a hole in my shoes when I was a lad, I suppose that is what you must expect when you buy your clothes "holesale".

Do you recall the old Max Miller classic: "When I was a kid, we were so poor we could not afford to wear shoes, so Dad blacked our feet and laced up our toes!" Now that story is not quite so silly as it sounds, for all kinds of dodges were tried in the old days to provide some form of footware. If your shoes or boots had holes in them, old pieces of paper or cardboard were inserted to block them, and if you did not have any footwear at all, Mum would wrap your feet with old pieces of blanket and tie them on with string. This may have looked strange, but it was better than running around the streets in bare feet during the winter months, a common practice for many of the poorer kids in the community, especially in Portsmouth during the early years of this century. Thank goodness there were a number of kindly folk who formed organizations to improve this sorry situation, they were generally referred to as Boot Funds. Much credit must be given to the *Portsmouth Evening News* for the boot fund that it instigated, bringing relief to hundreds of poor families in the area. The fund was still going strong at the outbreak of war in 1914, and in that year a room was obtained by the *News* in the old Arundel Street Council School. On Wednesday evenings hordes of young applicants would queue outside the school in the hope of gaining something to put on their feet, and it is interesting to recall that this fund even attempted to cater for little cripple children who urgently needed surgical boots.

Still on the theme of helping the poor, there was a son of Portsmouth who will always be remembered for his good works in this sphere, John Pounds. Although by profession he was a cobbler, John was distressed by the number of uncared-for children that ran about the streets, so he set himself the task of teaching them to read and write. As he was too poor to purchase books for this purpose, he secured advertisement bills from hoardings and made them into primers for his children. He induced the street urchins to come to his humble workshop by promising them hot potatoes, and with the ever-present pangs of hunger in their stomachs they needed little persuasion. John Pounds was born in Portsmouth in 1766, he began working life as an apprentice in the Dockyard, but through an accident he was made a cripple for the rest of his life, thus forcing him to set up as a cobbler in order to earn a crust of bread. Try to imagine the scene in the cobblers shop, John with a needle or hammer in his hands, surrounded by a group of poor children whom he endeavoured to teach the basics of some form of education that might some day help them to escape from their squalid surroundings. As I have mentioned in a previous section, young Billy Baker was one of his last pupils. John Pounds was as fond of birds as he was of children, and often expressed a wish that he might die like one, by dropping off his perch. His wish was granted, for one day he called at the house of a friend in the High Street, Edward Carter, and suddenly dropped down dead while waiting in the hall. He was seventy-three.

John Pounds must have had plenty of competition in his trade, for White's informs us that there were at least 150 boot and shoe makers operating in Portsmouth in the middle of the last century.

A rather surprising figure when you take into consideration that a good portion of the population could not afford to wear any footgear, and had to resort to walking the streets barefoot. One of the most notable boot and shoe establishments of that time appears to have been run by the Voysey family, for they had four branches in operation at the same time, they were sited in Sackville Street, Albion Place, Grigg Street, and Grosvenor Street.

One of the oldest shoe concerns still in operation must that of Bishop Brothers, I am pleased to say that at the time of writing they still have four branches flourishing in the area. It all began with James Bishop, who first came to Portsmouth in the 1890s to start his shoe chain here. James was already well-known in the city of Southampton, where he had in fact served as Mayor on two occasions, in 1884 and in 1889. It did not take him long to settle in Portsmouth, for by 1892 he was serving on the Portsmouth Council. His shoe establishment featured very prominently in Commercial Road, but after James Bishop died in 1913 the business expanded considerably, even crossing the harbour to take over George Blake's drapery and outfitting emporium on the corner of Bemister's Lane in Gosport.

One name that we cannot possibly miss off our list is that of George William Corbin, for the title of "Corbin" was displayed on the fascias of at least seven shoe branches in Portsea Island alone at one time. Following close behind was another George, for George Oliver had three branches in Portsmouth, and although the shops at Albert Road and King's Road have disappeared, a store in Commercial Road is still going strong. Akin to most of the other large towns and cities in the country, Portsmouth has enjoyed the presence of many revered shoe names trading in its midst, names such as Stead & Simpson, Saxone, Freeman Hardy & Willis, Milward's, John Farmer, and Gange & Sons. I do not have space to mention a fraction of the smaller traders, but given the choice of two I would mention Dick's Boot Stores in Charlotte Street and Commercial Road, and William Druce's shop in Meon Road, Milton. The latter, which only closed in 1982, was operated until its closure by Bill Druce. He had taken it over from his father William Druce, who originally opened the shoe repairing business in 1911.

Right, so there you are, fully outfitted from head to toe, and my goodness, you do look smart! What's that, you feel tight around the collar? I'm sorry about that, that was the trouble with the old separate shirts with stiffly starched collars. When you look at those old group photographs of handsome moustached gents with ruddy expressions, it was not because their cheeks had a healthy outdoor glow, it was because in actual fact they were choking!

Before we leave this floor, I would like to explain to you why you occasionally hear someone exclaiming "Ouch" at the top of their voice. These were the cries of tall unsuspecting store assistants being clonked on their heads by the overhead cash pulley system, reminding them that you had to be alert at all times. This system always fascinated me, money requiring change would be placed into a wooden or metal cup, screwed onto a cap and whisked away on an overhead wire to a counting house somewhere in the unseen corners of the store. In later years some stores replaced this with the air shaft system, you placed the money and bill of goods in a steel cylinder and placed it through flap, it was then transported to the accounts section by air suction. A minute or so later there would be a loud "clonk", informing us that the receipt and change had returned in the cylinder. Of course the pulley cash system was not only confined to drapery and tailoring establishments, or departmental stores for that matter, it was also used in larger food shops, generally the open type used by fishmongers. I used to hate this, for the change you received always smelt fishy, and the pong lingered for hours after!

Now, if you would like to follow me to the lift, we shall rise to higher things on the next floor.

Second Floor
Furnishing – Hardware – Wallpapers & Paints

I don't know, how times have changed! Setting up home today is a vastly different kettle of fish than it was years ago, few prospective brides and grooms of today are satisfied with presents such as ashtrays or toast-racks, and fridges and washing machines appear with expensive regularity on wedding lists. Many appear to start off their married lives with all the luxuries under the sun, including colour television sets. Although what a newly married couple would want with a colour television set, or even the black and white variety, I just cannot imagine!

It is a far cry from the old days, usually after you had got married you had to live in a rented flat furnished with orange boxes. Then if you were very careful, after a couple of months you might have saved up enough money to buy a piece of lino for the bedroom floor. But, we were happy enough, I suppose we did not know any better. Personally, I feel that this was a good thing, for if you have to work and save hard for something I think that you appreciate it all the more.

Mind you, when you could finally afford to buy it, the furniture of days gone by certainly lasted longer than that made today, there was none of this chipboard rubbish that passes for furniture now, it was always good solid oak or mahogany. The beds were decidedly more robust in those days, well they had to be really, for our Victorian and Edwardian predecessors certainly gave them plenty of use, as the large families of those times will testify. In some cases housing accommodation was so bad that entire families were forced to sleep in one room, and very often in the same bed. This reminds me of the silly story about the couple who had ten children living in one room and sleeping in one bed, it was such a common occurrence for the kids to fall out of bed, they all donned little crash helmets with their nighties. One night when the whole family were in bed, the husband turned to his wife and uttered: "Darling, do you realize that we have been married ten years, and you still look as lovely as the day we first met". At this, the eldest lad called out: "Look out kids, hang on to your crash helmets, here we go again!"

If you wanted a sturdy bed at a reasonable price, the place to go was the furnishing store of E. Curtiss in St. James's Road, where for the modest sum of £1.3.9d. you could become the proud possessor of a bed, with no previous owners! Of course, if you were really flush and fancied something a little superior, a super-duper de-luxe ornate brass job could be yours for £3.12.6d. Before you dash out of the door, I will remind you that these are 1914 prices! If I had been around then I think I would have put my money into beds, for those old brass bedsteads can now fetch hundreds of pounds!

Another place to visit in 1914 in order to furnish your home might have been the large furnishing store of Silverman's in Elm Grove, in fact they billed themselves as the largest furnishing store in Portsmouth, and with a shop frontage of 140 feet their claim probably had some justification. But when one begins to study this sort of claim in wider perspective, it seems that every store purported to be the largest store in Portsmouth, so perhaps it was just as well that the trade descriptions act was not with us then.

But Wallace Ash can certainly be included amongst the big boys, his huge premises in Russell Street could bear witness to this, and the title of emporium is well justified in his particular case, for he appeared to sell just about everything from bedroom suites to bicycles. The Ash store also stocked a large array of glass and china, so you may imagine the pandemonium that erupted one day in 1922 when they had an unscheduled visit from a bull. The animal was being herded past the Guildhall when it suddenly

Chaplin & Co.

"Deliveries Daily"

Curtiss of Southsea.

Parks of Portsmouth.

Handley's.

Debenhams.

1980s

Knight & Lee.

Vollers.

Allders.

bolted, and eventually swept in blind panic through the open doors of the Wallace Ash store. Talk about a bull in a china shop, after creating a scene of utter devastation, it backed through the plate glass windows at the front of the store. It eventually calmed down and was recaptured, leaving the staff of Ash's to sweep up the pieces. Wallace Ash was quite a character, and it is to his credit that he opened the first sewing machine shop in Portsmouth, and was also the first to fix rubber tyres to prams, so all babies should give a vote of thanks to dear old Wallace. The sewing machine really was one of the most wonderful inventions. Although early attempts had been made as far back as 1755 in England by Charles Weisenthal, it was left to a Frenchman named Barthelemy Thimmonier from Lyons to take the credit for inventing the sewing machine in 1830. Although this French tailor died in poverty in 1857, his invention continued to prosper, with the Singer company being formed in 1850. By 1900 over 20 million sewing machines were being produced each year, and you can be sure that Wallace Ash sold his fair share. Wallace served on the council and did a great deal of good work for the community, it was a sad loss to Portsmouth when he died in 1934 at the age of 90. In my collection of old bill-heads, I have a permanent reminder of the Wallace Ash establishment, dated 1904, it really is a marvellous work of art and well worth framing. But then, even with such a minor item as receipt pads or letter headings, the traders of days gone by displayed more flair and imagination than their modern counterparts.

Frank Spickernell certainly had plenty of flair and imagination, in fact many of the more sober citizens of Portsmouth thought he had too much at times. After serving for eight years in the Royal West Kent Regiment, Mr. Spickernell came to Portsmouth and started a furniture factory and showroom in Lake Road, and it is for this reason that he is included in this section, for I am sure that many older readers furnished their first homes with Spickernell furniture. Frank Spickernell also featured in *The Cinemas of Portsmouth*, another popular book in the **Down Memory Lane** series, for he put a great deal of faith in the cinema boom of the 20s and 30s by building the Plaza, Regent, Tivoli, and Troxy picture houses. It was through his sense of adventure and showmanship that the first talking film was shown in Portsmouth, and the first Sunday film programme was introduced. The latter raising a storm of protest from churchgoers. As Councillor Spickernell he twice served as Lord Mayor of Portsmouth, his first term in this position being in the Coronation Year of 1937. The city lost a tireless worker for good causes when he died in 1948, a year that must be included in the Golden Years of the Cinema, so perhaps it is just as well that Frank was not around to see the demise of cinemas in Portsmouth to the current sad state of affairs that now exists. Having said that, such was the business acumen of Frank Spickernell, he would probably have been the first to start a chain of video tape stores in the city.

Wendover's of Southsea has been furnishing homes in Portsmouth and Southsea for many years, and I am pleased to say that it is still flourishing from its revered establishment in Palmerston Road. It has always specialized in high quality merchandise, and serving the more affluent residents of Southsea it has continued to maintain its fine record for service and tradition. But unfortunately, the days have long passed when you could get carpet for 2/11d. a yard at Wendover's.

In the inter-war years Portsmouth developed into a formidable shopping centre, thus attracting many national chain-store names. Jay's Furnishing Stores first came to Portsmouth in 1928, opening a large store in Commercial Road. By that time Jay's had 130 furnishing stores spread around the country, the first one having been founded in 1884. Still in Commercial Road and only a few doors away from Jay's, was the Hampshire Furnishing Company, and but a few doors along was Kingswood & Marie on the corner of Thomas Street who were also house furnishers.

The furnishing establishment of Alfred Jacobs was also very popular, its main shop was in Commercial Road at the Rudmore end, but it also had branches in Elm Grove and London Road. More furnishing names from the past include Jepps & Co in the High Street, the Southsea Furnishing Company in Elm Grove, Whitmore Jones in Albert Road, Humphrey's in London Road, Hutchings in Albert Road, and White & Lowery in Fratton Road. We must also remember that most of the large departmental stores such as Handley's, John Dyer, L.D.B., and Knight & Lee also sold furniture.

When Father Painted the Parlour

I mentioned earlier those people who think they can do the other chap's job just as well as their own, for this is truly the age of "Do-it-Yourself". I don't mind having a go at little jobs around the house, although I cannot pretend that they are always perfect. I think the main consideration is to keep the "little woman" at home happy, even if your wallpapering is full of bumps and wavy edges, you can be sure that she will still usher the neighbours into the house to proudly proclaim: "Look, my Bert's just done this room." To which the neighbour will usually reply: "Oh yes, very nice, you are lucky to have a handy hubby," then retire back to their own house to collapse in hysterical laughter on the settee!

My old Dad was a typical home handyman, his wallpapering was unbelievable, the walls generally ended up looking like a relief map of Outer Mongolia. But his *piece-de-resistance* was painting window frames, this meant that we looked out on a snowy winter's scene all the year round! Mind you, in my opinion the finest invention for many years just has to be non-drip paint, for whenever the wife now says "That white paintwork is looking a little yellow," I give her a paint pot and a brush and reply: "There we are dear, it's all yours!"

Portsmouth has always sported a large number of stores where we could obtain our hardware and decoration supplies, and in the following paragraphs I shall attempt to recall some of them. Let us begin with Barnes & Seager, a business that was originally established in 1844 by a house decorator named Joseph Barnes. When Joseph had decided to hang up his paintbrush, the business was carried on by his son Robert. Robert Barnes was also involved in council affairs, and was destined to serve as Mayor. He will be remembered for his good work in setting up a relief fund for local families who had suffered losses in the terrible H.M.S. Victoria disaster. When he died in 1911 his place as head of the firm was taken by his son Henry, who very shortly after this went into partnership with Mr. John Seager, who had worked for Barnes for many years. Under their guidance the business expanded rapidly, the house decorating side being transferred to Palmerston Road, and a new showroom opened in Commercial Road.

In 1914, this showroom was one of the largest of its kind in Portsmouth, stretching back almost to Fountain Street. Over 25,000 rolls of wallpaper were generally kept in stock, I might add that they were mostly British papers, for the printing then of British papers was cleaner, softer, and better looking than those produced by foreign mills. In earlier times folk were quite content to pay 2d, or sometimes as much as 3d. for a roll of wallpaper, but by 1914 they were displaying a greater degree of taste, and had no objection to paying the huge sum of 8d. per roll! The Spendthrifts! At that time Henry Barnes was the Chairman of the company, and Harold Seager, the son of John, was the Manager. By the 1930s there was a split, with Barnes & Son carrying on their decorators supplies business from their Commercial Road showroom, and Harold Seager was operating as a paint and wallpaper merchant in Fratton Road. I think most of us are aware of the dangers of storing paint, so it is not surprising to learn that when Barnes paint shop in Commercial Road caught fire in 1936, it was one of the biggest blazes that Portsmouth had experienced. But of course, worse was to follow a few years later in 1940. Forty years on, I am pleased to say that Barnes & Son is still retailing wallpapers and paints, the main branch in Fawcett Road, and another in Gosport.

For your building supplies another popular establishment was that of Southey in Russell Street, this was founded by a gentleman named Allen in 1874, and was taken over by Mr. Southey in 1893. From then on the name of the game was expansion, and by the outbreak of the 1914–18 war they had four warehouses and two workshops in Sussex Street and three showrooms in John Street. Southey's had expanded from an original staff of three in 1893, to a workforce of over 60 in 1914. That new wonder known as electricity was beginning to make it's mark, and Southey Limited was responsible for several large wiring contracts, including the Municipal Institute, and the St. Saviour's and Ascension churchs in North End.

W.P. Winter & Son, another well known name, still trades from showrooms in Blackfriars Road. One of the oldest builders merchants in Portsmouth. Winter's also deals in timber supplies, and this is a service for which our next Portsmouth trader is renowned throughout the area, W.H. Wheeler & Sons. W.H. established the business in 1877, his interest at that time being lath rendering, just one facet of the timber industry. But the introduction of the sawn lath led Mr. Wheeler to turn to timber trading on a large scale, and by the time that he had opened his premises in New Road in 1899, he was well established as a timber merchant. His sons followed him into the business, his grandsons, and even his great grandsons, and the name of Wheeler for timber and Do-it-Yourself supplies is known throughout the Portsmouth area, including branches in Fareham and Gosport.

I like looking at old photographs of hardware shops, it always amazed me how much stock that they could pack on to the pavement outside, just about everything from rolls of lino to dustbins. It must have taken hours to take it all out, and just as many to take it back in when it came to closing time. There are still a few of these establishments carrying out this practice, but I am afraid that it is a trait that will disappear in the future, the chief objection being the obstruction of our pavements, a constant source of complaint from blind folk.

In recent times we have seen the disappearance of a much-revered Commercial Road store that always had plenty of stock on the pavement, the surplus supplies store of Ben Grubb. The Grubbs were a Portsea family, and it was in Queen Street that Ben Grubb opened a second-hand furniture shop in 1907. Around 1931 he moved to the Mile End area of Commercial Road, but the site was taken over later for the new Savoy Cinema, so he moved to 362, Commercial Road. These premises were bombed, and they had to carry on the business in various places. Then in 1968 they moved to 344, Commercial Road, a shop that had previously been used by the aforementioned Barnes, and before that it had served as a Gospel Mission Hall. Ben died in 1946 at the age of 60, and the business was carried on by his son Ron Grubb. It is interesting to know that Ben had a son named Ben, who also had a son named Ben, but neither of them entered the business.

By now, it would have become obvious to most readers that almost any trader of note served at one time or another on Portsmouth City Council, and they may have noticed that many of them became Mayor. George Couzens was one of this select band, in fact he served as Mayor of Portsmouth for three terms of office. Away from the council chamber George was kept busy running the family hardware and ironmongery business in Commercial Road, for he had succeeded his father in running this popular store. He worked hard for the business and in public life, and it did not appear to do George Couzens any harm, for he died at the age of 73 in 1925. Dealing in the same line of business, we must not forget another George who served Portsmouth as Lord Mayor in the 1950s, George Day. Cutting the blue and yellow ribbons with a pair of gold scissors at Handley's entrance in 1955 was just one of the many highlights in George Day's term of office, other events included meeting the Princess Royal, the Duchess of Gloucester, Queen Elizabeth the Queen Mother, and a visit to Buckingham Palace for the Queen's Garden Party. It would be true to say that he was Lord Mayor at a time when Portsmouth was beginning to emerge from the gloom of the aftermath of war, and starting to see the fruition of its rebuilding programme. Dealing in builders materials, the firm of G.A. Day made its contribution to that programme, and I am pleased to report that its trade is still flourishing in the 1980s, with a large showroom at Burrfields Road and a branch in West Street, Fareham.

The next hardware establishment on our list could also have been included in the section on chemist shops, and by this subtle clue I am sure that most readers will have realized that I am referring to that revered household name, Timothy White's. Sadly, this name is disappearing from our high streets, for in 1983 it was announced that most branches will have closed by 1984. It all began with one very ambitious young man, Timothy White, who came to Portsmouth in 1848 to found a oil and saltery business in Portsea, he was 23 years old. Serving the Dockyard folk, he did well, and was gradually able to expand by adding household goods and medicines to his range. He opened his first retail shop in Chandos Street, rapidly followed by another in Palmerston Road, and subsequently hundreds more over the following fifty years or so. Timothy gained the title of Major through his association with the 2nd Hants Artillery Volunteers, he was one of the pioneers of this movement. He was very generous and did much good work on behalf of the Landport Ragged Free School, and was sadly missed when he died in 1908. The business was carried on by his son, Sir Woolmer White, who had qualified as a pharmacist. Under Woolmer the Timothy White concern underwent further expansion, then in 1928 it merged with Taylor's the cash chemists, a large chain store group run by Philip Hill. Hence the title "Timothy Whites & Taylors". After the war, it opened one of the most modern stores of 1951 in Palmerston Road, and bargain opening offers included white enamelled buckets for 4/6d., ironing tables for 27/11d., and hot water bottles for 3/9d. But to push the knife in even deeper I will remind readers of Timothy White's prices in the pre-war years: how about a 21-piece tea service with coloured borders for 2/4d., or a 40-piece set for 8/11d. Ruby decanters were 11½d. each, and glass fruit dishes from one penny each. Canary cages sold for 2/11d., gas rings for 10d., and carpet sweepers for 8/6d., Mind you, that was a lot of money, so most folk used a carpet beater, yours for 4d. "Wow", talk about "Sale of the Century"! I suppose you could say that it was the beginning of the end for Timothy Whites when it was bought out in 1968 by Boots.

I am afraid that I shall now have to bring this section of the book to a close, but here are a few more ironmongery names from the past to remember. Taylor's in Marmion Road was an old established firm, and it flourished for over 100 years from the early 1800s. Then there was Bowerman Brothers in Osborne Road, Albert Barber in Albert Road, H.A. Evans in Goldsmith Avenue, Hooper's in Kingston Road, Perryman's in St. Mary's Road, Waldron & Son in Chichester Road, and Walker Morley in Commercial Road. I think the halcyon year for Portsmouth ironmongers must have been 1881, for this was the year of the Great Snowstorm, when a roaring trade was enjoyed in shovels and brushes. The snow was so bad that none of the local traders could open their shops, and it was days before anyone could get out of their houses. This also meant good business for the firm of John Palmer in Somers Road, for he was the founder of the brush-making industry in Portsmouth.

Bargain Basement

We have now reached the point in the book where in an attempt to please as many people as possible, I will throw in just about everything but the kitchen sink. Not that we need a kitchen sink, for I bought one in the last section when you were not looking! This is also the part of the book in which we might pick up a bargain, and I don't know about you, but I have always been a sucker for bargains. In fact, I think I was reading *Exchange & Mart* even before the *Gem* or *Magnet*. I was always sending off money in reply to adverts that proclaimed such startling statements as "Do people Look Down On You? Send Away Now For Our Unique System, You Can Be Taller In 14 Days". This was generally followed by testimonials from clients such as "M.S. of Tooting", who gained three inches in four weeks, or "Miss A.V. of Scunthorpe", who keeps knocking her head on the lampshade after only three weeks! I followed the course religiously for six months, casting aside pain and agony as I lay on my bed whilst Mum and Dad pulled like crazy on my feet and arms to stretch me to King Kong proportions! Needless to say, I actually lost half-an-inch in height, and people were able to look down on me from an even greater height!

In days gone by the place to get a bargain in Portsmouth was in the famous Penny Bazaar in Commercial Road, the forerunner of the Woolworth 3d. & 6d. Stores. The Bazaar was a veritable Aladdin's Cave for young eyes, for everything was priced at one penny. As fantastic as it may seem now, that meant that you could buy 240 items for a pound! The assistants working in the Penny Bazaar had to be a pretty hardy bunch, for it was completely open at the front with no windows for protection, and it remained open well into the evening even in wintertime.

Considering the price limitation it was quite amazing what a vast variety of goods were offered. As far as the kids were concerned, the most important part of the Bazaar was the toy counter, and offered for the sum of one penny were dolls, skipping ropes, toy soldiers, whips and tops, pencils and chalks, penny whistles and toy trumpets. For the Billy Bunters of this world there was also a sweet section, and for one penny you could get enough sweets to keep even the most ardent young scoffer happy for several hours. And while you were munching your toffee apple, Mum was also busy in the Bazaar looking for bargains, and bargains there were, from mops to floorcloths, from carbolic soap to meat skewers, and from button to collar studs. All for a penny!

The official name of this great bargain store was the "Premier Penny Bazaar", and there was a branch in Southampton. I have already mentioned how prices went up in the First World War, so it is not surprising that after it they could not keep up to their name, but the same theme was carried on by Woolworth's hence the 3d. and 6d. tag that this world renowned chain store carried in the pre-1939 years. In America, where F.W. Woolworth's originated, the shops were known as "Five and Ten Cent" stores. This vast commercial empire was founded in 1879 by a former shop assistant named Frank Winfield Woolworth, and I very much doubt that when he opened his first modest little store in New York he could have possibly imagined the fantastic size that his off-spring would attain. The first Woolworth store in Britain was opened in 1909 in Liverpool, ten years before F.W.'s death at the age of 67, and it was not long before most of the large towns and cities in the country could boast a Woolworth branch in their High Street, Portsmouth had two Woolworth stores, one in Commercial and the other in King's Road. The latter branch was almost next to John Dyer's great emporium in the 1920s, but by the 1930s they had moved down to Elm Grove. In the 1980s the Commercial Road store still overlooks the busy precinct scene, and the Southsea branch flourishes in Palmerston Road.

Stores of the Woolworth type were referred to in directories as bazaars, and under this heading we must include another well-known High Street name, Marks & Spencer, which like Woolworth's has been in evidence for many years in Portsmouth, in fact for well over fifty years. Other bazaars in the 20s and 30s included the Domestic Bazaar Company in Commercial and King's roads, and the establishment of S. Karmy in King's Road.

Those were the days when it was a case of "short-back-and-sides" when you went to the barbers for a haircut, for it was essential to have short hair in the long-running battle against the dreaded nits. Ugh! Just typing that word makes me feel like scratching! Not everyone could afford to pay 3d. or 6d. for a haircut, so it was a case of sitting on a stool in the kitchen with a pudding basin on your head whilst Mum whipped around with a pair of scissors. the only problem was that your cap fell over your ears for weeks after! At one time there were over two hundred hairdressers cutting a living in Portsmouth, and it is notable that many of them were old-established family businesses. May I remind you of just two, the Folland's and the Knipe's. The former had four hairdressing salons spread around Portsmouth, and these were run by Albert, Henry, Arthur, and William Folland. Knipe's was the larger though with at least seven shops, and flashing away with the comb and scissors we had George, William, Alfred, and Selina Knipe, assisted by an assortment of sons.

My favourite hairdressing story in Portsmouth concerns Houdini, the great escapologist. Harry Houdini was over here on a tour, and was packing large audiences into the Hippodrome in Commercial Road for one week. Ever conscious about his appearance, during his stay he paid daily visits to a barbers shop in nearby Russell Street for a shave and a trim, I believe it was Percy Stringer's salon. Anyway, Houdini was so pleased with the service that he received, he presented the barber with a special sign that more or less indicated that the "Great Houdini" had been shaved there. The sign was placed in the window and there it stayed for many years. Although Houdini died in 1926, he was to make one of his most amazing escapes some fifteen years later in 1941. Following that dreadful raid of January the 10th, the area around the old Hippodrome was reduced to rubble, a mass of broken glass and bricks. But there, amongst the devastation that had once been a hairdressers, lay the original Houdini advert, intact and unscratched! Houdini Had Escaped Yet Again!

Just imagine the confusion that could be caused by a bomb falling on a pawnbrokers shop, and going back to the shop on Friday morning to redeem your best suit and finding the place completely flattened, brass balls and all! Having a good suit was quite an asset in days gone by, for if you were short of a bob or two you could always pop around to "Uncles" and put it in pawn. Some looked on pawnbroking as an act of providence, so perhaps it was not purely by chance that Portsmouth's biggest pawnbroker, the establishment of Baker & Co., was sited in Commercial Road on the corner of Providence Path. I say biggest because Baker's had six branch shops in the city, the most widely used proving to be the shop in Queen Street.

If you lived in the Arundel Street or Surrey Street area, the friendly smiling pawnbroker to whom you passed your ticket over the counter at regular intervals, was probably named Fulljames, for both John and Tom Fulljames operated there beneath the sign of the three brass balls. Certainly they were in business to help themselves, but in many ways pawnbrokers were carrying out a public service. Tom Fulljames took this a step further, for he served for 43 years on the Council, during a period when Portsmouth underwent vast development. He ran his pawnbroking shop for over 60 years, and helped to form the Portsmouth Branch of the National Association of Pawnbrokers in 1890. He died in 1929 at the age of 80.

Complete with eyeshades and huge magnifying glasses, at one time there was something in the region of thirty pawnbrokers making a living in Pompey, and some of their names included the Hewett Brothers in New Road and Blackfriars Road, A.W. Couzens in St. James Road, Arthur Frank Roberts in St. Mary's Road, Parnell & Roberts in Guildford Road, Bennett & Son in Eldon Street, Freake & Son in Twyford Avenue, and George Hunter in Meadow Street. But my favourite pawnbroking name from the past just has to be that of Caleb Nancarrow, who had three shops doing good business, namely in Church Road, Kingston Road, and Highland Road.

Apart from suits, some of the most frequent items to pass back and forth over the pawnbroker's counter were wedding rings, and this very nicely leads us onto the subject of jewellers. There can be little doubt that, when one contemplates the value of gold, silver, and jewellery now, those who were fortunate enough to have the money in the old days were certainly able to make a good investment by a trip to the jewellers shop. The chief problem about owning a jewellers store is the vulnerability of your merchandise from the evil clutches of thieves and crooks, for a brick through the window could cost you thousands of pounds. How many times have you heard a burglar alarm bell clanging away outside a jewellery store in the High Street? And have you noticed, nobody appears to take a blind bit of notice about it! I like the robbery report listed in a *Hampshire Telegraph* of 1815, it states: "Last evening, about seven o'clock, a fellow thrust his hand through a pane of glass in the shop window of Mr. Hough, the Portsmouth jeweller, and snatched a small tray containing gold and ornamental rings. But, such was his hurry, many of the rings fell into the street, and he only got away with merchandise worth ten to twelve pounds, his pursuers picking up the rest". I don't know about the thief, I wonder if the pursuers were ever seen again!

The jewellery firm of H. Samuel has been around a mighty long time, and it has operated from the same site in Commercial Road for many years. But, one of the oldest establishments still operating is that of Pickett & Purser in Palmerston Road, founded in 1850. In the pre-war years, Mr. Thomas Pickett and Mr. John Purser had separate stores in Commercial Road. I particularly like Purser's advertisements of 1915, showing a very modern approach to thumping their soapbox, they billed themselves as the "Ring-Leaders".

Another of the absolute gems from my billhead collection is a receipt issued by Millward & Co. of King's Road in 1905, the engraving is really superb. The receipt itself records the sale of a "Silver English Lever Watch", the sum paid being four pounds. This really was a quality timepiece in 1905, for in those days you could get a pocket watch for only five bob! Another billhead, relating to G. Dimmer the jeweller in Palmerston Road, is for only 1/6d., this being the charge for a small adjustment on a clock. But the portion of the heading that catches my eye, is the part that announces that Mr. Dimmer is the official "Chronometer Maker to the Admiralty and the Indian Government".

Casting aside such merry quips as "Can you buy clocks on Tick"? I will surge on with more jewellers names from the past. Edward Kirkman had jewellery stores in Elm Grove and The Arcade, Owen & Son in Lake Road, George Whitfield in Palmerston Road, Henry Daley in London Road, John Jackson in Palmerston Road, Fleming in Castle Road, Edgar Stocks also in Castle Road, Reginald Price in Albert Road, Warne's also of Albert Road, and finally Albert Fielder in Commercial Road.

The mention of billheads reminds us of the important part that printers play in the world of commerce, for although none of us like receiving bills, someone has to print them. Apart from bills, think of all the window stickers, handbills, showcards, and general printing work that may be included in the transaction of buying and selling goods. The printers of yesterday took a great pride in their work, treating it more as a work of art than an everyday item, thus making some of their printed work valued collectors pieces today. The Portsmouth name that appears to stand out from the rest is that of Charpentier's in the High Street, for they flourished in this thoroughfare for over one hundred years. The business was founded by William Henry Charpentier in the 1830s, he was a talented artist who made drawings of every building in the High Street in order to preserve a record of the changing face of Portsmouth. This old established printing business was very much associated with the subject of history, for they produced guide books, maps, prints and postcards that spanned a century. The drawings executed by the Snape family, notably William and Martin Snape, were produced in profusion by Charpentier's, and have been used to illustrate a multitude of local history books, including **Down Memory Lane** publications. Alfred Moth was married to Agnes, the youngest daughter of W.H., and on returning to this country from America, where he had started a tobacco plantation, Alfred acquired the Charpentier business on the death of Ernest Charpentier in 1892. Alfred and Agnes produced two sons and three daughters to carry on the name. The Charpentier empire was regretably brought to a sudden and sickening end in 1941, a victim of the German bombers. Sadly, apart from the machinery being completely destroyed, irreplaceable historical drawings were also lost forever.

Alfred Moth died in 1922, and in that same year Portsmouth lost another popular printer, William Henry Barrell. Starting at the bottom of the business, William rose from apprentice to manager, and subsequently to boss of this High Street printing concern. In later years William was also prominent for his work in the Portsmouth Chamber of Trade and Commerce. Like Charpentier's, Barrell's also produced many local history books and guides that have become collectors items.

Mention of the fine work produced by the Snape family in capturing old Portsmouth on board and canvas, reminds me of an artist who also carried out invaluable work in this field, the talented Richard Ubsdell. He was well known for his early paintings of the town and the local area, he also carried on a miniature and photographic business at No. 1 Green Row, but he actually resided in the house of Vicat Cole for a number of years. Between 1833 and 1849, Richard had five pictures exhibited at the Royal Gallery. It is believed that his last picture was painted in 1870, the subject being his beloved Governor's Green.

Richard Ubsdell did not have far to go to have his pictures framed, for the frame-making establishment of Albert Gardner was in Pembroke Road, and had been there since 1857. They also dealt in Fine Art, and in later years one of their specialities was the sale of paintings and etchings by the great maritime artist, W.L. Wyllie. William Lionel lived in Tower House by the mouth of the harbour, and apart from his marvellous artistic work, will be remembered for the prominent part he played in ensuring that H.M.S. Victory was restored after she was brought out of the harbour in 1922.

What is that? All this name-dropping has given you a headache, don't worry, what you need is a headache powder. It is lucky that we are still in Old Portsmouth, for just around the corner in the High Street is one of Portsmouth's most famous chemists. No Madam, not Mr. Tremlett, he will follow later, for the moment I am dealing with the shop of William Saunders. Apart from his prowess as a chemist, William Saunders was also a noted historian, and wrote a fine piece of work titled the *Annals of Portsmouth*, an important contribution to local history. He also had an extensive historical collection, and generously donated many pieces to Portsmouth Museum, the old building that was situated in the High Street. Serving on the Town Council from 1876, Portsmouth lost one of its finest characters when William Saunders died in 1913.

Funeral arrangements by G. Andrews, 1922. Stephen Brading leads procession.

In the latter half of the last century approximately forty chemists dealt out their magic potions in Portsmouth, and apart from Mr. Saunders and the aforementioned Timothy White, not many of these names survived into this century. In the 20s and 30s there were some seventy chemists battling it out on Portsea Island, armed with pestles and mortars. By this time our old friend Mr. Tremlett was well and truly established, for he had opened his first shop at the turn of the century in Fratton. Percival Gordon Tremlett came from the Isle of Wight, and crossed to Portsmouth to serve an apprenticeship in the pharmaceutical trade, following which he started up on his own account. The rest is history, and over the years Tremlett's became more of an institution than a chemists shop, especially for the poorer folk who lived in the Fratton area. No matter what you had wrong with you, earache, headache, backache, toothache, or just plain nits, a miracle cure would be passed over the counter for a few coppers. The Workers Educational Association Local History Group in Portsmouth have produced an interesting little booklet written by Richard Tremlett, the founder's son, entitled *Sixty-two Years a Fratton Pharmacist*. It is full of humorous anecdotes relating to the business, and I would highly recommend it to local history addicts. Of course, the Tremlett name is still well in evidence in the Portsmouth area, and includes branches in Gosport and Portchester.

Chemist Frederick Gall died in 1936, as he had reached the ripe old age of 89, it is evident that he was very well known in Portsmouth, especially in the Arundel Street area where he had his shop. Residents who lived at Eastney were well taken care of through the chemists shop of John Arkell in Eastney Road, whilst those in the Copnor district could all upon the services of Cyril King in Hayling Avenue. A few more chemists names might include Arthur Goddard in Twyford Avenue, Tom Fox in Commercial Road, Frank Glanville in Haslemere Road, Napier's Pharmacy in New Road, William Bown in Victoria Road North, William Parsons in Chichester Road, Sydney Rogers in Osborne Road, and not forgetting Boots the Cash Chemists, with branches everywhere. But I take off my hat to all chemists, both old and new, for with their magic cure they probably do more to keep the nation moving than prune-juice. Mind you, many of them recommend the latter in any case!

I will never forget those old "Monday Washday Blues", with poor old Mum sweating it out over a steaming boiler with a copper stick in her hands, there was none of your super-duper automatic washing machines about then! They certainly prayed for good drying days in the old days, for many families had only one set of clothing, and the kids had to stay in bed until their togs could be brought in dry off the washing line. Most folk only had small backyards, so this restricted the length of the clothes line somewhat, with Dad's woollen long-johns monopolizing the proceedings.

I suppose that there are still a few folk who use an old roller wringer to get the water out of their clothes after washing, but generally these worthy appliances seem to have vanished from the modern washday. When I was a nipper we had one of those great cast-iron mangles with a large wheel for turning, when it came to passing through blankets you would have had to have reached Lesson No. 6 of your Charles Atlas Course to even start the handle turning. But, as a kid it was more than just a mangle to me, for with a strong imagination you could stand at that wheel and pretend that you were Captain Hornblower steering a huge sailing vessel through a storm in the China Seas, or maybe Malcolm Campbell wrestling with the steering wheel of Blue Bird whilst breaking the world landspeed record.

Clothes washing was all part of life's hard grind in days gone by, and if your old man was out of work, many mothers were glad to take in other people's washing. This is something we do not see on our streets today, ladies scuffling back and forth with battered old prams loaded high with washing. Of course, some people had the money to send their clothes to the laundry, and these establishments did a good job by providing a great deal of employment for the working-class ladies of Portsmouth, for in those days laundries did not possess any fantastically automatic machines that render a human workforce redundant.

If you look in the Yellow Pages now you will find the list of local laundries is somewhat smaller than the number that existed forty to fifty years ago, but I am pleased to say that there is still at least one of the old names still in operation in the 1980s. I hardly have need to tell readers that I am referring to Chapman's Laundry in Kingston Crescent, for it has been around for nearly one hundred years, being founded in 1886. Chapman's has very little competition now in their particular field, apart from the home washing machine and laundrettes of course, but in earlier days its great rival was the Royal Laundry in Taswell Road. This laundry went back even further, it was founded in 1860 and was operated by the Hutchings family for many years. And not too far away from Chapman's was the Brunswick Family Laundry in Gladys Avenue, and the Farlington Laundry in Powerscourt Road run by Mr. Martin. Then there was the Southsea Laundry Company in Highland Road, the Hygeia Laundry in Fawcett Road, The Nelson Laundry in Malins Road, Fryer's Laundry in Admiralty Road, the Cottage Grove Sanitary Laundry, the Albert Family Laundry in Albert Road, the Westfield Laundry in Eastney, and the Warren Avenue Laundry in Milton.

Foremost on the list of tradesmen who had regular need of having their clothes washed must be chimney sweeps and coalmen, two more trades of which the numbers have become greatly reduced through people's reluctance to make up and clean out fire grates, preferring to flick on a switch. But you know, you cannot beat a good old coal fire, there is something about them that is more welcoming and homely.

If anyone has any doubts about the disappearing chimney sweep, let them consider that the Yellow Pages directory lists three sweeps in the Portsmouth area, whilst in the 20s and 30s there was something in the region of thirty to forty only too pleased to give folk the brush-off. Of those names the most prominent were those of the Boutler family who operated from the Southsea area, and the Eneas family, with Charles working from Hyde Street, and Herbert from Leopold Street. We might also include Charlie Prevett in Wilson Road, Ernie Boys in Chilcote Road, George Ketchlove in Grenville Road, and William Bailey in Chapel Street. Chimney sweeps do not have too much to celebrate nowadays, but they certainly did in times long gone, I have already mentioned in a previous section about the Chimney Sweeps annual festivals that took place near Pink's Corner in Commercial Road.

When it comes to Portsmouth coal merchants the name that most readers will quickly recognize is that of J.E. Smith, although I believe they have merged with Corralls in recent times. They have operated from their main office in Goldsmith Avenue for many years, and have spread to other areas such as Fareham, Gosport, and Waterlooville. James Edward Smith is another trader who carried out good work on the city council for many years, and in 1929 he became Lord Mayor. Away from the council chamber he was a staunch member of the Salvation Army, and his four sons and six daughters were also closely involved with this worthy organization. Not many people realized that Alderman Smith had a secret ambition, as a young man he desperately wanted to join the police force, but unfortunately could not pass the medical. However, in later years he was able to serve as a special constable in the 1914–18 war, and found that he did not like police life after all, in fact he was jolly glad that he had not been accepted all those years before! J.E. Smith died in August

1951, surviving two wars.

William Lawrence had died some years prior in 1929, as he was 83 he was acknowledged as one of the oldest coal merchants in Portsmouth. Lawrence & Co. had branches in Fawcett Road and Copnor Road. Fraser & White were also spread well around the district, as were J.R. Wood & Co, their main depot being in Rudmore. Mention of Fawcett Road reminds us of coal merchant William Boxall, still going strong into the 1980s. Boxall's was originally in Beatrice Road. More coal names include Arthur Colverson in Burgoyne Road, Arthur Dewey, Clements Brothers and Flowers & Co of Goldsmith Avenue, Jeram & Co of Copnor, Henry Purkis in Tipner, and the award for my favourite coal name goes to the Dockyard Impartial Coal Society in Fratton. With its close proximity to Fratton Railway Station, it is not difficult to understand why Goldsmith Avenue was a favourite spot for coal merchants to site their depots.

Perhaps we appreciated coal fires more in the old days because it was generally the only form of heating in the house, and only in the living room. Thinking back, the only time a fire was lit in the bedroom was when somebody was ill, central heating was virtually unheard of then. Since those days, I think we have all got a bit softer, in fact I am sure that we have. Still, as I always say, I won't have to worry about heating bills when I die, for where I am going it will be mighty hot, according to parsons anyway! Mention of dying brings us to our last department in the Portsmouth Emporium, I just had to save it for the end of the book, for you cannot get more final than death. Not in this life anyway!

No matter what state the country is in, whether it be recession or depression, the undertaking trade will never lack for customers, for when the Good Lord calls, then you have just got to go! Generally the fun begins after the funeral, with relatives whom the deceased had not seen for many years, suddenly appearing out of the woodwork to see if their name was mentioned in the will!

Shirtmaker, Commercial Road.

Commercial Road.

What always amuses me is the way that the dearly departed's belongings are shared around within hours of the funeral. "Now look here Lil, there is a suit hanging up in Harry's wardrobe that would fit your Fred a treat, and he had some underwear in his drawers that was brand new, never been worn"! This explains why people who went back to the deceased person's house after the funeral for a cup of tea or a glass of cheap British Sherry, always leave with beaming faces and carrier bags crammed with old clothes!

The arguing about who should get this or that, or about who should not have got this or that, is not always put aside until the dead person has had the final spade of earth tossed over them at the graveside. I have a report of a very strange scene that was enacted at Highland Road Cemetery in the 1920s, when a group of relations were standing around the hole in the earth. One mourner made a rather nasty remark, and within seconds a heated verbal exchange was taking place over the grave. The deceased's daughter fainted by the graveside, a relative was stooped looking after her when he was struck in the back by another relative, causing another relative to retaliate. A right ding-dong ensued around the grave, and it was an absolutely amazing scene, certainly one that the gravediggers of Highland Road Cemetery had never seen before! It ended with all the mourners appearing in court, and I can only surmise that the late head of the family was up in Heaven laughing his head off!

As I have mentioned previously, most of the large departmental stores such as Knight & Lee, Handley's, John Dyer's, Morant's, and Wendover's operated a funeral department, and I believe that Knight & Lee only ceased providing this service in 1961. Many firms appeared to have taken on undertaking as a sideline, their usual trade being building or cabinet making, or perhaps something far removed from the funeral business. But when we start remembering Portsmouth undertakers, the award for being the

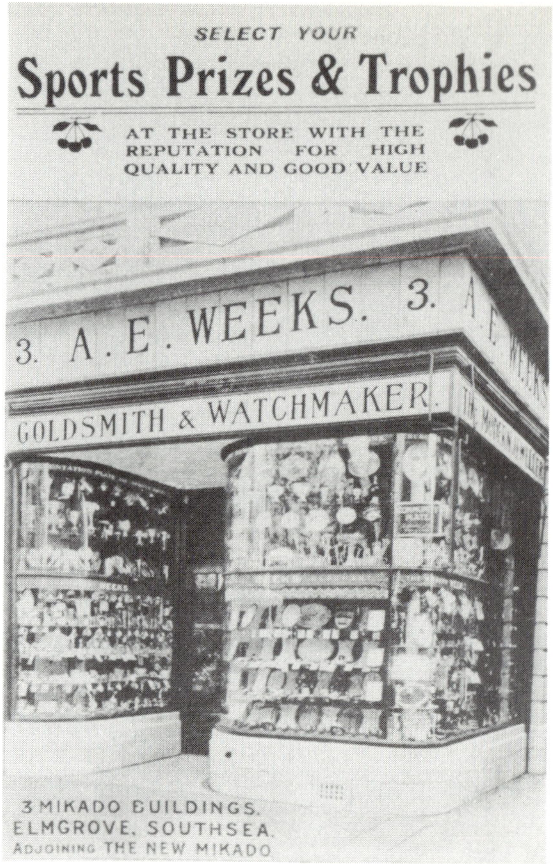

oldest established business still flourishing must go to G. Andrews & Son at Kingston Crescent, although in actual fact it has not been run by the Andrews family for over sixty years. It all began with George Andrews who founded the business in the last century, operating from Hanover Street until they settled in the well known establishment at Kingston Cross. When George had need of his own services, the business was carried on by his son, William Henry Andrews, William was very much tied up in council affairs, and for his good work he was promoted to the rank of Alderman in 1938. He had relinquished his interest in the funeral trade long before this, for in 1921 G. Andrew & Son was taken over by the Brading Family, notably Stephen Brading. His son James made the business his career, and when Stephen Brading died in 1960 he took over. In the 1980s, James still has an interest in the business as Governing Director, and his brother Eric Brading looks after the day to day running of the firm.

Leading undertakers today include Barrells in Fratton Road, the Co-operative Funeral Service, also in Fratton Road, and Dashwood and Denyer in St. James's Road. The name of Dashwood is also associated with earlier times, for Dashwood & Sons operated from St. James's Road for many years. There were also Harris & Son in Gladys Avenue, Gordon Norgate in Somers Road, Fred Roberts in Arundel Street, Bill Savage in Powerscourt Road, Alf and Ebb Stapleford, and Arthur Thompson in Albert Road. I might add that A.G. Stapleford & Sons are still going strong in Powerscourt Road.

I will conclude on a more cheerful note by reminding readers about a few Pompey folk who kept the undetaker waiting, for although the general opinion is that people in the old days did not live to a great age, there is always the odd exception to this rule. For instance, take the case of David Davies who worked in the Dockyard for most of his life, he was 105 years old when he died in 1803. Then there was old seaman George Gregory, who went to meet his Maker in 1804 at the ripe-old age of 109. But the prize for longevity goes to Tom Botwell, who sold water in the Portsmouth streets, for when he finally kicked the bucket in 1818 he was 113 years old! Another remarkable fact is that Tom was married to the same woman for eighty years, she ending their loving partnership at the age of 101! There must have been something in the water that Tom Botwell sold!

That concludes our look at shops and businesses as such, but there is another aspect of retailing that I would like to devote my last columns to, the world of advertising. Generally, getting the sales message across can play a vital part in the success of a business, for it does not matter how many fantastic bargains you have crammed into your establishment, if the public do not know about them, there is no point in opening.

The rather strange facet about advertising, is that it very often relies upon traders who are not enjoying good business. Let me explain. When business is good, there is not so much urgency to advertise, but when trade is slow, then something has to be done to attract the customers. This is why, in times of recession, you will find that advertising space is at a premium. So, we may apply the old adage, "One Man's loss, is another Man's gain". Enter your friendly advertising representative!

Most of the old traders had a great deal of faith in the power of advertising, and it would seem that they never tired of having their name splattered all over town, that is why almost every available space was filled with posters telling us to go to "Fred Bloggs, the most honest, and the most reliable trader in town". Bill-sticking was a thriving trade in times gone by, with posters being fixed to anything that did not move, lamp-posts, fences, walls, bus and tram columns, and of course, the vehicles as well.

In recent times I have been pleased to see the old custom of advertising by sandwichmen revived, for it always amused me to see these chaps staggering across the pavement with huge boards strapped to their shoulders, with placards advising us to "Dine at Joe's Cafe". Whilst the sandwich boards were popular for getting the sales message across, on occasion they were used for messages of a more sobering kind, such as "The End Of The World Is Nigh".

How many times do you hear people say: 'I don't know, the newspapers are full of nothing but adverts"? This may be true to a certain extent, but the cold facts of life are that newspaper concerns would have to pack up tomorrow if it were not for the advertising. Without adverts, our daily papers would probably cost about £1 a copy!

In my opinion, by living in the area served by the Portsmouth *News*, we are fortunate in having available one of the finest newspapers in the country. *The News* provides its readers with an interesting mixture of world, national, and local news. It also allows regular space in which readers may let off steam, and air their views on local affairs and happenings. As far as Portsmouth traders and businessmen are concerned, they have long realized the value of *The News* as a showcase for their wares.

Before I expound further on the history of the Portsmouth *News*, let us have a look back at some of the paper's predecessors. The history of newspapers in Portsmouth goes back to the middle of the 18th Century, but it was not until 1799 that a permanent press was established in the area, this heralding the introduction of the *Hampshire Telegraph*. When it first appeared on October the 14th, 1799, it was called the *Portsmouth Telegraph*, or *Mottley's Naval and Military Journal* as an alternative title. I am fortunate enough to have in my collection two copies of the *Hampshire Telegraph* dated 1805, and apart from interesting news of Lord Nelson's meeting with Mr. Pitt, plus news of Napoleon's latest exploits, I find the adverts particularly fascinating, occupying as they do some 30 per cent of the paper. It was printed and published at that time by Mr. J.C. Mottley, at the Telegraph Printing Office, Portsmouth.

The *Hampshire Telegraph* did not have a great deal of competition in the first half of the last century, there were several attempts to establish other journals, but most of them were doomed to failure. Until the mid-1800s, newspaper circulation and the sale of space for advertising was hit by taxation, but in 1853 relief came with the abolition of tax on advertising, then, a couple of years later the newspaper duty of 4d. a copy was withdrawn, and in 1861 the duty of 3d. a pound on paper was also abolished. So, from then on, it was all systems go, and the volume of advertising increased considerably.

The *Telegraph* had it's first serious rival with the *Portsmouth Times*, an excellent journal that first appeared on the Portsmouth streets on 30 March, 1850. It was to remain in existence for 78 years, almost to the day, for it was absorbed by the *Hampshire Telegraph* in March, 1928. Another paper to suffer a similar fate was the *Hampshire Post*, which first appeared in 1874, it was taken over by the *Hampshire Telegraph* in 1913.

Portsmouth did not have an evening newspaper until the 1870s, this being when the *Evening News* was published on 27 April, 1877, their premises being a former butcher's shop in Arundel Street. The paper, which sold for a halfpenny, was printed on a flat-bed press that was sited in what had previously been the butcher's slaughterhouse. The hand-set type was pieced together by six compositors, grafting away in a small upper room that had formerly served as a bedroom. There is no truth in the rumour that this is how the well-known phrase "Putting the Paper to Bed" originated.

A Scotsman, James Graham Niven, was the founder of the *Evening News* in Portsmouth. It would appear that the energetic Mr. Niven was involved in all aspects of the product, from going out and getting the news and adverts, to actually delivering it by cart. I am pleased to say that his efforts were well rewarded, for the original circulation had doubled to 4,000 within a short space of time. About this early stage in the history of the paper, a young man named William Gates joined the Niven organization, and it was his destiny to not only fill the Editor's desk for over thirty years, but also to make the biggest written contribution so far in recording the history of Portsmouth. In addition to scores of guidebooks and hundreds of articles on old Portsmouth, William Gates book *The History of Portsmouth* still stands as the most comprehensive work produced on the subject, and commands a considerable sum of money as a collectors item. Although he retired from the *News* in 1926, he remained active as a director of the company. William Gates died in 1946 at the grand age of 90.

William had taken over as Editor from Hugh Maclaughlan, who had held the post since 1883. That particular year was significant in that it saw the demise of Mr. Niven, who sold out to a group of newspaper pioneers formed by Samuel Storey, Passmore Edwards, and Scottish-American millionaire Andrew Carnegie. Continuing their policy of acquiring newspapers all over the country, the trio had already bought the *Hampshire Telegraph*. Not long after their arrival on the newspaper scene in Portsmouth, the partnership was dissolved when Edwards and Carnegie left to concentrate their energies upon other projects, thus leaving Samuel Storey in control.

The *Evening News* found a formidable rival in 1884 when the *Evening Mail* was launched in Portsmouth, re-named the *Southern Daily Mail*, it was eventually taken over by the *Evening News* in 1905. The *Southern Daily Post* was just one of the local papers that tried to emulate the success of the *News*, but like the rest it was short-lived. It began printing on 29 August, 1911, from a new press installed at premises in Fratton Road, and although full of "Southern Promise", it ceased publication after only five months, on January 27th, 1912.

By 1895 the Arundel Street premises had become too small for the expanding *Evening News*, so they moved lock stock and barrel to a new building in Stanhope Road. They were to remain there until August, 1969, when operations were moved to spacious premises at Hilsea, known as The News Centre. At the same time, the *Evening News* title was replaced by *The News*, and the tabloid format reverted to broadsheet. Covering over 100,000 households throughout Hampshire, West Sussex, and the Isle of Wight, *The News* still flourishes as the premier provincial newspaper in the South, and is still the most popular media for advertising. And why not, what was good enough for the Bulpitt's and Handley's of yesteryear, is good enough for the Debenhams and Allders of today.

My only regret was the passing of the dear old *Hampshire Telegraph* in November, 1976, after 177 years, the proprietors, Portsmouth and Sunderland Newspapers Ltd., regretfully withdrew it from publication after issue number 10,102. This was not only a sad blow to the papers many regular readers, it was a great loss to local historians, for it had covered Portsmouth area events from the reign of George III. Like *The News*, it was not just a newspaper, it became a way of life.

Early days in King's Road.

Lane's, the cheapest meat in town.

Closing Time

The shop assistants are waiting to cash up, so we must now close the doors of the Portsmouth Emporium. I sincerely hope that readers have enjoyed our nostalgic ramble, and deem this modest work worthy enough to be given a permanent position on their bookshelves. Preferably next to other books in the **Down Memory Lane** series!

During the pleasant task of compiling the facts, figures, and photographs for the book, I count myself fortunate to have been afforded the help and assistance of several people. I am indebted to Lorna Poole, Archivist of the John Lewis Partnership, to Mr. Hayward and Miss Keetch of the Portsea Island Co-op Publicity Department, Joan Kenton and to Jackie Facy, Cyril Stares and Henry Bowditch for their personal reminiscences. Many of the pictures that illustrate the book are extremely rare, I would therefore like to thank my old friends Alf Harris, Bill Buckley, and Pru Read for letting me dip so freely into their private collections.

And so, we pull down the shutters on the Portsmouth Emporium. I am sorry if I did not mention your favourite trader from the past, but I am sure that most readers will realize that I cannot possibly get thirty quarts into one pint pot, for that is the sort of task that the subject demands. Nevertheless, I will be pleased to receive any reminiscences or photographs from readers via the publisher, and who knows, one day I might produce **The Portsmouth Emporium II**. In the meantime, "Happy Shopping".

Franklin's Grocery Store, Commercial Road, c.1914.